TABLE OF

Top 20 Test Taking Tips

MASS 6

Introduction 6

Test Format 7

Scoring 7

On the Day of the Exam 8

How to Use This Guide 8

Assembly 10

Mechanical Concepts 13

Reading Comprehension 27

Mathematical Usage 30

Background and Opinion Questionnaire 42

Practice Test 44

Practice Questions 44

Mathematical Usage 44

Reading for Comprehension 47

Assembly 55

Mechanical Concepts 61

Answers and Explanations 76

Mathematical Usage 76

Reading for Comprehension 77

Answer Key 80

Assembly and Mechanical Concepts 80

Secret Key #1 - Time is Your Greatest Enemy 82

Pace Yourself 82

Secret Key #2 - Practice Smarter, Not Harder 82

Success Strategy 82

Secret Key #3 - Prepare, Don't Procrastinate 83

Secret Key #4 - Test Yourself 83

General Strategies 83

Special Report: How to Overcome Test Anxiety ... 89
Lack of Preparation ... 89
Physical Signals ... 89
Nervousness ... 91
Study Steps ... 92
Helpful Techniques ... 94
Special Report: Retaking the Test: What Are Your Chances at Improving Your Score? ... 98
Special Report: Additional Bonus Material ... 100

Top 20 Test Taking Tips

1. Carefully follow all the test registration procedures
2. Know the test directions, duration, topics, question types, how many questions
3. Setup a flexible study schedule at least 3-4 weeks before test day
4. Study during the time of day you are most alert, relaxed, and stress free
5. Maximize your learning style; visual learner use visual study aids, auditory learner use auditory study aids
6. Focus on your weakest knowledge base
7. Find a study partner to review with and help clarify questions
8. Practice, practice, practice
9. Get a good night's sleep; don't try to cram the night before the test
10. Eat a well balanced meal
11. Know the exact physical location of the testing site; drive the route to the site prior to test day
12. Bring a set of ear plugs; the testing center could be noisy
13. Wear comfortable, loose fitting, layered clothing to the testing center; prepare for it to be either cold or hot during the test
14. Bring at least 2 current forms of ID to the testing center
15. Arrive to the test early; be prepared to wait and be patient
16. Eliminate the obviously wrong answer choices, then guess the first remaining choice
17. Pace yourself; don't rush, but keep working and move on if you get stuck
18. Maintain a positive attitude even if the test is going poorly
19. Keep your first answer unless you are positive it is wrong
20. Check your work, don't make a careless mistake

MASS

Introduction

Congratulations! You've decided to take the Power Plant Maintenance Positions Selection System (MASS) examination, which means you are pursuing employment as a power plant maintenance worker. This is an excellent career move, for a number of reasons. For many people, this kind of hands-on, active job is a perfect fit. Power plant maintenance workers get to move around and work in a variety of different locations; they have a number of different responsibilities throughout the course of the day. Maintenance workers work both independently and in groups as part of a team. Additionally, because power plant maintenance workers receive specialized training, they can be highly paid and receive excellent career benefits for their services.

Despite all of the physical and financial rewards of a career in power plant maintenance, many individuals find that meeting the mental challenges of the job is more satisfying. Power plant maintenance workers are constantly required to solve problems both great and small. In order to ensure that a power plant is running smoothly, a huge number of calculations and adjustments must be made on a daily basis. For this reason, a power plant maintenance worker must be adept at considering the various aspects of a problem and imagining realistic and viable solutions. Sometimes, the options available to the worker will be limited by resources; when this is the case, a power plant maintenance worker has to be creative in improvising a solution. Therefore, despite outward appearances, the work of a power plant maintenance worker is as much mental as physical.
Another benefit to choosing power plant maintenance is the variety of tasks with which one can be tasked in this field. The responsibilities of a power plant maintenance worker include all of the following: testing and repairing equipment; installing new parts; installing insulation; supervising the work of others; training subordinate employees; planning large-scale projects and maintaining adequate supplies. As you can see, this encompasses a wide range of physical, administrative, and organizational tasks. All of these jobs, however, require the same basic skills. In order to succeed in power plant maintenance, you will need to be able to read with understanding, make quick mechanical assessments, solve basic math problems, and perform arithmetical calculations.

The Power Plant Maintenance Positions Selection System (MASS) examination is designed to measure your knowledge and skill in these areas. This exam is primarily taken as part of the application process for employment at a large energy company. However, a high score on the MASS exam can also be a great way to bolster your resume as an independent contractor. Success on the MASS exam indicates that you have the knowledge and skills required to tackle a multitude of problems. It also indicates that you are serious about making a career in this field.

Unfortunately, many would-be power plant maintenance workers miss out on a great career because they are intimidated by the idea of sitting for a written examination. Many associate standardized tests with their time in school and want to avoid the experience in any way they can. It is true that some of the topics covered on the MASS exam are similar to those found on more academic tests, like the SAT. However, the material on the MASS is specifically adapted to be relevant to individuals interested in power plant maintenance. Furthermore, in the assembly and mechanical concepts sections of the exam, the MASS focuses exclusively on problems that are likely to be encountered in the course of employment as a power plant maintenance worker. Many test-takers find that they actually enjoy solving these problems; after all, it is this pleasure in learning how things work that has led them to this field in the first place.

In any case, there is no reason why you should not succeed on the MASS exam. With the right kind of preparation, you can guarantee yourself a great score. This guidebook has been written as a comprehensive primer to the MASS exam. It contains detailed information about the content and types of questions you will encounter on examination day. After you have spent some time reading this book and practicing the kinds of exercises to be found on the exam, you should have no problem achieving an excellent score!

Test Format

The Power Plant Maintenance Selection System (MASS) exam consists of four aptitude tests and a background and opinion questionnaire. The four aptitude tests cover the following areas: assembly, mechanical concepts, reading comprehension, and mathematical usage. The assembly section tests your ability to mentally envision the form of an object after it has been properly assembled. This section of the exam consists of 20 multiple-choice questions, which must be completed within ten minutes. Each question is followed by five possible answers.

The mechanical concepts section measures your ability to comprehend the basic principles of mechanics. This section of the exam consists of 44 multiple-choice questions, which must be completed within 20 minutes. Each question is followed by three possible answers.

The reading comprehension section of the exam measures your ability to obtain information and make inferences based on expository texts. It consists of 32 multiple-choice questions, each with four possible answers. You must complete this section within thirty minutes.

Finally, the mathematical usage section assesses your ability to solve basic arithmetic problems. It consists of eighteen multiple-choice questions, each accompanied by five possible answers. You will have seven minutes in which to complete this portion of the exam.

In all, the MASS exam should take only a couple of hours to complete. You must complete the sections in the order in which they are given, and you will not be allowed to go back to a section once you have completed it. It is a good idea to bring your own pencil to the exam site, though extra pencils and scratch paper will be made available to those in need.

Scoring

The scoring of the MASS exam is a relatively simple matter. You will be given four individual scores for each of the four aptitude sections of the exam (the background and opinion questionnaire is not scored). These raw scores will be based on the number of questions you answer correctly. The graders of the MASS exam do not distinguish between unanswered questions and questions answered incorrectly, so you should always take your best guess when uncertain of a particular answer. The four scores will be combined to produce an Index Score on a scale from 1 to 10. For all intents and purposes, this Index Score will be the record of your performance on the MASS exam. There is no minimum passing score recommended by the exam administrator; it will be up to your employer to judge your scores. Most scores fall between 3 and 8; both extremely low and extremely high scores are rare.

On the Day of the Exam

When you register for the MASS exam, you will be given detailed information on where and when the examination will be given. The MASS exam is administered at testing facilities around the country; oftentimes, the exam will be administered by a large employer as part of the application process.

No matter where or when you take the exam, there are a few things you can do to maximize your performance. First, and perhaps most importantly, get a good night's sleep before your examination. You do not want to be groggy when you sit for the exam. Also, if you are taking the exam in the morning, be sure to eat a complete and balanced breakfast. Research consistently suggests that jumpstarting the body's metabolism with an early meal increases blood flow to the brain. Being hungry or weak from lack of food can inhibit your ability to concentrate during the exam. If you are taking the exam later in the day, bring a healthy snack (like a banana or a granola bar) to eat right before you begin. Also, be sure to drink plenty of water; like hunger, dehydration can make it difficult to focus your attention. Finally, be sure to wear clothes that are comfortable as well as appropriate for the testing environment. You will want to make a good impression on the test administrator, but you also want to wear clothes that will not distract while you work.

How to Use This Guide

This book endeavors to be a comprehensive guide to the Power Plant Maintenance Positions Selection System (MASS) examination. It covers in detail all of the content and question types that will appear on your examination. It may be, however, that you are already fairly knowledgeable in one of the areas covered by the examination. If you are a math expert, for instance, you may already know much of the information covered in the mathematical usage section. For this reason, do not feel that you have to read this book from cover to cover. Feel free to concentrate your study on those areas of the examination for which you need the most preparation. If you have a limited time to study before the exam, focus your efforts on the content areas which are least familiar to you, as it is in these areas where you will see the most immediate improvement.

Moreover, you should not try to read this book in its entirety without interruption. A great deal of information has been condensed here, and it would be nearly impossible to retain all of it from a single reading. Here and there, we have indicated practice exercises which you can use to supplement the information contained in the book. Practicing the skills described herein is the best way to solidify your knowledge. Also, performing some practice exercises will accustom you to the type of thinking that you will have to do on the exam itself.

The best way to use this book in preparation for the MASS exam is to read a little bit at a time for several weeks before testing. If you can read and practice a small amount every day, you will steadily acquire all of the knowledge and skills you need to ace the exam!

Assembly

To begin with, let's take a look at the assembly section of the MASS exam. Many test-takers find that they feel most comfortable with this section of the exam because it plays to their natural strengths. Aspiring plant maintenance workers are likely to be people who enjoy taking things apart and putting them back together; working with their hands to get a sense of how machines are assembled. This section of the test measures your ability to imagine the way an object will look when its pieces are joined together properly. The 20 multiple-choice questions that make up this section will begin with a picture of five separate parts. Each of these parts will be marked with one or more letters. These letters will be assigned to places on the part. Sometimes the letter will appear directly over part of the object, and sometimes a line will be drawn from the letter to the appropriate spot on the object. If there is a dotted line drawn from the letter to the object, this means that the letter corresponds to a place on the side of the object that cannot be seen. Your task will be to imagine how the object will look when all of the parts are connected such that the letters touch one another. In other words, all of the parts marked with an *A* will need to touch; all of the parts marked with a *B* will need to touch, and so on. You will be given five assembled objects from which to choose your answer. This format will be the same for all twenty questions in the assembly section.

The format of the assembly questions, then, is fairly straightforward. However, you will only be given 10 minutes to solve these twenty problems, and therefore you will need to be able to work efficiently. This means approaching the assembly questions with a strategy in mind. There are a couple of different ways to proceed. Perhaps the best way to approach assembly questions is to proceed in order and work methodically. In other words, begin my mentally connecting the *A*s; once you have this assembly in mind, move on to the *B*s, and so forth. One mistake that many test-takers make is to attempt the entire assembly all at once. Many of these problems will involve four or five parts, and it will be too easy to get confused if you do not work in order. Indeed, the test administrator will be sure to include a few close-but-incorrect answers designed to trip up people who work too fast. The best way to proceed through an assembly question is to firmly decide on the arrangement of the object one piece at a time.

In tandem with this strategy, you can use the process of elimination to quickly reduce the number of possible answers. After you have mentally connected the *A*s, for instance, you can go through and rule out all of those answers that do not have the *A*s connected properly. You can then proceed through the Bs, ruling out a few more answers, until you are left with a single possible right answer, which you can then take a moment to confirm.

There are a few things to keep in mind when considering possible solutions to an assembly problem. To begin with, remember that the pieces can be turned in any way. They may be rotated, spun, and flipped. They may not, however, be folded, bent, or twisted. Furthermore, they may not change in size; each piece should be the same size in the answer as it is in the original picture. Occasionally, the makers of the MASS exam will place the pieces in the correct configuration but will drastically alter the sizes of one or more pieces. This automatically invalidates the answer. It is best to imagine the pieces as solid three-dimensional objects, which can be manipulated in all directions but cannot have their fundamental size and shape altered.

Similarly, make sure that the answer you select has the appropriate number of pieces. If there are five different components in the original drawing, there must be five connected parts in the answer. It is common for the exam to leave out a piece or include an extra piece in one or more of the possible answers; even if these answers are right in all other respects, they cannot be correct if they include more or fewer pieces than the original drawing.

Once you have worked through the problem in this systematic manner and have selected your answer, go back and double-check your work. To begin with, make sure that all of the letters are joined properly in the answer you have chosen. Then, make sure that your answer has the right number of pieces. Finally, make sure that the pieces in the assembled object are similar in size to the pieces in the original drawing. If all of these factors check out, you can be comfortable that you have selected the right answer.

This methodical way of working through assembly problems may seem too time-consuming given the limits of the exam, but with a little bit of practice you can speed through the process within the time given. In fact, by adhering to this organized way of solving assembly problems, you will actually save time, since you will never get confused or lost in a problem and have to go back to the beginning. All it takes to master these problems is a little strategic knowledge and a little preparation. Having covered the strategy, let's now take a look at a few ways to prepare for this section of the exam.

There are a few common activities you can use to prepare for the assembly section of the exam. For instance, even though jigsaw puzzles do not offer an exact replication of the items you will encounter on the MASS exam, they still exercise your spatial reasoning skills. Envisioning which pieces of the puzzle will fit together, and how the resulting arrangement will look, is a great way to hone your assembly skills. For an even greater challenge, try turning all the pieces of the puzzle face down, so that you cannot use the picture to guide your work: this will force you to rely more on your sense of orientation and arrangement.

Another way to prepare for this section of the exam is to take apart a small piece of machinery and study its configuration. Yard sales and junk bins are great places to find old appliances and electronics equipment. With the help of a screwdriver, wrench, and pair of pliers, you should be able to take apart most any appliance with ease. Once you have broken the item down into a pile of parts, see if you can put those parts back together into a functional whole. Even better, have someone else take apart the item and then see if you can put it back together. Of course, it is not recommended that you try this with valuable or expensive pieces of hardware. Also, some electronic appliances contain small batteries which should not be handled by non-professionals; always obey any warnings listed on the equipment. Nevertheless, taking apart and putting together small machines can be a fantastic way to improve your assembly skills.

Finally, there is a wealth of spatial intelligence exercises to be found on the Internet. Just by entering "spatial intelligence" into a search engine, you should receive listings for dozens of simple, free puzzles and games that strengthen your ability to visualize and perform basic assemblies. Some of these programs are so sophisticated that they allow you to manipulate three-dimensional objects on your computer screen! While for many people working on a computer is no substitute for direct contact with an object, these on-line exercises are a clean, fast way to stretch your mental muscles.

Whatever method you choose, be sure to prepare for at least a few hours before sitting for the MASS examination. For most students, the most difficult thing about the assembly questions is getting comfortable with the format and learning how to approach the problem. By remembering the strategies discussed above, and utilizing some of the suggested practice exercises, you can make sure that you will be ready to attack assembly problems immediately.

Mechanical Concepts

For most MASS test-takers, the mechanical concepts section of the exam is the most appealing. People who are interested in power plant maintenance often have an intuitive sense of the physical world, the behavior of machines, and the best ways to accomplish a physical task. All of these areas are covered in the mechanical concepts questions. This section of the exam consists of 44 questions, and must be completed within 20 minutes. This may not seem like a great deal of time, but many of the questions will not require more than a few seconds of thought once you have solidified your understanding of the basic concepts of applied physics and mechanics. Each of the 44 questions will be based on a picture, and will have three possible answers. The pictures will contain all of the information required to answer the questions. Some of the questions have to do with specific machines, while others apply mechanics to more general topics.

In order to succeed on the mechanical concepts section of the MASS exam, you will need to be familiar with basic concepts in physics and mechanics. Don't worry: the MASS exam does not dwell on obscure theories or require you to make complicated calculations. The equations that are included in this section of the book are meant to illustrate the relationships of physics, not to show you how to solve numerical problems. You do, however, need to understand the essential properties of physics, and how they apply to real-life situations. In order to help you along, we have included a full primer on all of the concepts that may come up on this section of the exam. Important terms and concepts are placed in bold. Finally, although we have tried to make this section of the guidebook as easy to read as possible, we still recommend that you take your time and avoid reading in a hurry. You may need to read some of this information a few times before fully absorbing it. Whenever possible, try to imagine some everyday examples for the concepts we discuss; after all, applying the theories of physics to the materials of everyday life is one way to define mechanics.

Displacement

To begin with, we will look at the basics of physics. At its heart, physics is just a set of explanations for the ways in which matter moves. When something changes its location from one place to another, it is said in physics to have undergone displacement. If we can determine the original and final position of the object, then we can determine the total displacement with this simple equation: *Displacement = final position – original position*. Displacement along a straight line is a very simple example of a vector quantity: that is, it has both a magnitude and a direction. On the MASS exam, you will probably not need to distinguish between vectors and scalars (quantities without direction); however, you should understand that direction is as important as magnitude in many measurements.

Velocity

In order to solve some of the problems on the exam, you may need to assess the velocity of an object. If we want to calculate the average velocity of an object, we must know two things. First, we must know its displacement: the distance it has covered. Second, we must know the time it took to cover this distance. Once we are in possession of this information, the formula for average velocity is quite simple: *average velocity = change in position / change in time*. In other words, the average velocity is equal to the change in position (final position – original position) divided by the change in time (final time – original time). This calculation will indicate the amount of distance that was covered in each unit of time. If time stays the same, then velocity goes up when distance goes up. When distance stays the same, velocity goes up when distance goes down.

Note that there is a difference between velocity and speed. Oftentimes, people without training in physics confuse the words 'speed' and 'velocity.' There is a significant difference. Whereas a measure of the average velocity is concerned with the amount of displacement, a vector, the average speed is only concerned with the distance covered. That is, a measure of average speed does not contain any information about the direction in which the object is traveling. For this reason, average speed can be calculated: *average speed = total distance / change in time* (notice that we used total distance and *not* change in position, because speed is only concerned with scalar quantities). On the MASS exam, velocity and speed will be essentially interchangeable.

Acceleration

Acceleration, meanwhile, is the change in the velocity of an object. To calculate average acceleration, we may use this simple equation: *average acceleration = change in velocity / change in time.* Acceleration will be expressed in units of distance divided by time multiplied by time; for instance, meters per second squared. If the time remains the same, the acceleration will increase as the change in velocity increases. If the velocity stays the same, the acceleration will increase as the change in time decreases.

Newton's three laws of mechanics

The questions on the exam may require you to demonstrate familiarity with the concepts expressed in Newton's three laws of mechanics. Before Newton formulated his laws of mechanics, it was generally thought that some force had to act on an object continuously in order for it to move at a constant velocity. This seems to make sense: when an object is briefly pushed, it will eventually come to a rest. Newton, however, determined that unless some other force acted on the object (most notably friction or air resistance), it would continue in the direction it was pushed at the same velocity forever. In this light, a body at rest and a body in motion are not all that different, and, indeed, Newton's first law makes little distinction. It states that a body at rest will tend to remain at rest, while a body in motion will tend to remain in motion. On the MASS exam, you are likely to see some questions that ask you to consider the various properties of bodies in rest and bodies in motion; for this reason, we need to take a look at force, mass, and friction.

Force

Let's take a moment to examine the concept of force in some detail. A force is something that gives acceleration to somebody. Force is a vector; that is, it has both mass and direction. This can be demonstrated by considering an object placed at the origin of the coordinate plane. If it is pushed along the positive direction of the *y*-axis, it will move in this direction; if the force acting on it is in the positive direction of the *x*-axis, it will move in that direction. But if both forces are applied at the same time, then the object will move at an angle to both the *x* and *y* axes, an angle determined by the relative amount of force exerted in each direction. In this way, we may see that the resulting force is a vector sum; that is, a net force that has both magnitude and direction. On the MASS exam, this distinction can emerge in problems which ask you to determine what will happen when objects moving in two different directions collide. The objects will move in a direction somewhere in between their original direction. A larger or faster object will exert more force on the other object, and will therefore have a post-collision path closer to its original path.

Mass

A number of questions on the MASS will require you to consider the results of applying a certain amount of force to a few different objects. If we apply the same force to two objects of a different size, we will often find that the resulting acceleration is different. The reason for this is that the two objects have a different mass. Mass is typically defined as the quantity of matter in an object. The relationships between force, mass, and acceleration are outlined in Newton's second law of mechanics. This law is generally written in equation form: *Force* = *mass* x *acceleration*. In other words, as mass or acceleration increase, so does force. Of course, in order to competently apply this equation, you must be certain what body it is being applied to. This measure only includes those forces that are external to the body; any internal forces, in which one part of the body exerts force on another, are discounted. Newton's second law somewhat encapsulates his first, because it entails that if no force acts on a body, then the body will not accelerate.

Weight

Too often, weight is confused with mass. Strictly speaking, weight is the force pulling a body towards the center of the earth. The reason for weight is primarily a gravitational attraction between the masses of the two bodies. The SI unit for weight is the Newton. In general, we will be concerned with situations in which bodies with mass are located where the free-fall acceleration is g (in most earthbound applications, g is equivalent to the acceleration of gravity—32.2 ft/s^2 or 9.8m/s^2—hence 'g'). In these situations, we may say that the magnitude of the weight vector is: $W = mg$.

Normal force

The word "normal" is used in mathematics to mean perpendicular, and so the force known as normal force should be remembered as the perpendicular force exerted on an object that is resting on some other surface. For instance, if a box is resting on a horizontal surface, we may say that the normal force N is directed upwards through the box (the opposite, downward force is the weight of the box).

Tension

Another force that may come into play on the MASS exam is called tension. Any time a cord is attached to a body and pulled so that it is taut, we may say that the cord is under tension. This force is pointed away from the body and along the cord at the point of attachment. In simple considerations of tension, the cord is generally assumed to be both without mass and incapable of stretching. In other words, it's only role is as the connector between two other bodies. Even if both body and cord are accelerating, the cord is assumed to pull on both ends with the same magnitude of tension. This is also assumed to be the case in situations where the cord runs around a pulley (a scenario frequently seen on the MASS); unless circumstances are clearly or purposefully otherwise, pulleys are assumed to have both negligible mass and negligible friction.

Newton's third law of mechanics

This brings us to Newton's third law of mechanics. This law is quite simple: for every force, there is an equal and opposite force. When a hammer strikes a nail, the nail hits the hammer just as hard. If we consider two objects, A and B, then we may express any contact between these two as exactly the same, only in opposite directions. Although the two forces are often referred to as the action and reaction forces, in physics there is really no such thing: there is no implication of cause and effect in the equation for Newton's third law. At first glance, this law might seem to forbid any movement at all; we must remember, however, that these equal, opposite forces are exerted on different bodies with different masses, and so they will not cancel each other out. Part of your job on the MASS will be to decide in which direction the movement occurs, which you can do by considering the masses and velocities of the bodies.

Friction

A great number of the questions on the exam will require you to consider the forces that can prevent movement. These forces are generally known as friction. In order to illustrate the concept of friction, let us imagine a book resting on a table. As it sits there, the force of its weight is equal and opposite to the normal force. If, however, we were to exert a force on the book, attempting to push it to one side, a frictional force would arise equal and opposite to our force. This kind of frictional force is known as static frictional force. As we increase our force on the book, however, we will eventually cause it to accelerate in the direction of our force. At this point, the frictional force opposing us will be known as kinetic frictional force. For the most part, kinetic frictional force is lower than static frictional force, and so the amount of force needed to maintain the movement of the book will be less than that needed to initiate movement.

The mysterious force known as friction is really just the force exerted by the surface atoms of one object on those of another. In situations where extremely flat and polished metal surfaces are brought into contact with one another in a vacuum, friction can be so great as to effectively weld the pieces of metal together. Most of the time, though, even surfaces that appear flat to the human eye are not really flat enough to create that much friction. Instead, only the very tops of two surfaces will touch one another. As an object is pulled across another, millions of tiny ruptures will occur on a microscopic level, as the peaks of one surface are ground against the peaks of the other. For the purposes of the MASS exam, however, you should remember that flatter and harder surfaces tend to generate less friction.

Occasionally, a question will ask you to consider the amount of friction generated by an object that is rolling. If a wheel is rolling at a constant speed, then the point at which it touches the ground will not slide, and there will be no friction inhibiting movement. (Incidentally, the friction regarding the portion of the wheel touching the ground is in fact static friction, as there is no dragging, but a constant contact.) If, however, a force should act on the wheel, changing the speed of the center of mass or the angular speed of the wheel about the center, then the wheel may slide on the ground and be subject to friction. Until the wheel slides, the frictional force is static; once it slides, however, frictional force is kinetic. If a wheel is dropped onto an incline, the force of friction will actually propel it forward, as the sliding of the bottom of the wheel will encourage rotation. Indeed, when the rider of a bicycle pushes on the pedals to speed up, he or she is making use of the force of friction to accelerate.

In describing the basic properties of friction during contact between two bodies, we are assuming that both bodies are dry and unlubricated, and that a force is attempting to slide one body across the surface of the other. The first property of friction is that, if the body does not move, then the static frictional force is exactly equal and opposite to the force being exerted in an effort to move the object. Static frictional force has a maximum value, however. If the magnitude of the force that is parallel to the surface should exceed the maximum value of static friction, the body will begin to move.

Once a body has begun to slide along the surface of another, the frictional force will decrease. In other words, an object's kinetic frictional force will always be less than the maximum value of the static frictional force. This means that it is easier to keep an object moving than it is to set it into motion. This distinction is likely to be important on a few questions of the MASS exam.

Drag force

Friction can also be generated when an object is moving through air or liquid. A drag force occurs when a body moves through some fluid (either liquid or gas) and experiences a force that opposes the motion of the body and is exerted in the direction in which the fluid is moving relative to the body. The drag force is greater if the air or fluid is thick or is moving in the direction opposite to the object. Obviously, the higher the drag force, the lower the velocity of the object in motion.

Work

This brings us to the concept of work. The equation for work (W) is fairly simple: $W = Fd$, where F is the magnitude of the force exerted and d is the displacement of the object on which the force is exerted. The force vector and the displacement vector will usually have the same direction. If force and direction have the same direction, then work is positive; if they are in opposite directions, however, work is negative; and, if they are perpendicular, work done by the force is zero.

Kinetic energy

When we see an object in motion, we assume that work has been performed on it. The kinetic energy of the object is that quality of its motion that can be related in a qualitative way to the amount of work performed on the object. Kinetic energy cannot be negative. Changes in kinetic energy will occur when a force (F) does work (W) on an object, such that the speed of the object is altered. This change in kinetic energy is equal to the amount of work that is done. This relationship is commonly referred to as the work-kinetic energy theorem. If there are several different forces acting on the object, then "work" is simply the total work done by all the forces, or the net force.

One interesting exam application of the work-kinetic energy theorem is on objects in a free fall. To begin with, let us assert that the force acting on such an object is its weight, equal to its mass times g (the force of gravity). The work done by this force will be positive, as the force is exerted in the direction in which the object is traveling. Kinetic energy will therefore increase, according to the work-kinetic energy theorem. If the object is dropped from such a great height that it eventually reaches its terminal velocity (the point at which it can go no faster due to resistance), then the drag force will be equal to the weight, and so the total amount of work exerted on the object will be zero. According to the work-kinetic energy theorem, this means that the kinetic energy of the object will remain constant.

Power

On occasion, you may need to demonstrate an understanding of power, as it is defined in applied physics. Power, put simply, is the rate at which work is done. Power, like work, is a scalar quantity. Power can be calculated by dividing the amount of work performed by the amount of time in which the work was performed. If more work is performed in a shorter amount of time, more power has been exerted. Power is typically expressed in joules per seconds, more commonly as watts. Sometimes, it may be better to express the rate at which work is done in terms of the force and the velocity of the body. If this is the case, power may found as $P = Fv$, in which P is the instantaneous power and v is the speed of the object. This means that if force or velocity goes up, power will go up as well. On the MASS exam, you may see problems that ask you to decide whether more power is generated by a faster or more forceful collision.

Energy

Energy is a word that has found a million different uses in the English language, but in physics it really just refers to a measure made on one or more bodies. By assessing either its behavior or its configuration, we may be able to measure the amount of energy in a body or group of bodies. There are various kinds of energy: kinetic energy is associated with motion; potential energy is the energy associated with particular arrangements of bodies; mechanical energy is the sum of an object's kinetic and potential energy.

Potential energy

Potential energy is the amount of energy that can be ascribed to a body or bodies based on configuration. There are a couple of different kinds of potential energy. Gravitational potential energy is the energy associated with the separation of bodies that are attracted to one another gravitationally. Any time you lift an object above the ground, you are increasing the gravitational potential energy of that object. Another kind of potential energy is elastic potential energy; elastic potential energy is associated with the compression or expansion of an elastic, or spring-like, object. Physicists will often refer to potential energy as being "stored" within a body, the implication being that it could emerge in the future. The MASS exam may present you with problems that require you to indicate whether there is potential energy in a spring or compression system.

Mechanical energy

Mechanical energy is the sum of kinetic and potential energy. If a spring is compressed by a block hitting it with kinetic energy, it gains potential energy as the block loses kinetic energy. The change in energy is equal and opposite. The mechanical energy of the entire block-spring system is constant throughout. For another example, imagine a ball moving vertically perpendicular to the surface of the earth, with its weight the only force acting on it. As the ball rises, the weight will be doing work on the ball, decreasing its speed and its kinetic energy, and slowing it down until it momentarily stops. During this ascent, the potential energy of the ball will be rising. Once the ball begins to fall back down, it will lose potential energy as it gains kinetic energy. We can say then that as the ball rises energy is transferred from the ball to the ball-earth system, and as the ball falls energy is transferred from the ball-earth system back to the ball. In this relation, mechanical energy is conserved throughout; the potential energy of the ball at its height is equal to the kinetic energy of the ball at its lowest point.

In systems where friction or air resistance is negligible, it is easy to construct systems in which mechanical energy is conserved. However, if we take friction into account, we arrive at a different sort of result. For example, let us imagine a block sliding across the floor until it comes to a stop due to friction. Unlike a compressed spring or a ball flung into the air, there is no way for this ball to regain its energy with a return trip. Therefore, we cannot say that the lost kinetic energy is being stored as potential energy. Instead, it is dissipated, meaning that its transfer cannot be reversed. In general, we must admit that the mechanical energy of the block-floor system has been not conserved but reduced.

If we consider a block and spring system (in which a block slides against a spring which is compressed, and then returns to its natural resting state), we will see that the oscillations of the spring decrease until they become zero, as the spring returns to its resting state. This decrease in kinetic energy will happen as the thermal energy of the block and the ground beneath it both increase. For the purposes of the MASS exam, it is enough for you to realize that there is no loss of energy, though energy is transferred into different forms. This is only appropriate for an isolated system, however: in a strict sense, most systems will involve numerous additional energy quantities.

We have seen that energy, though it may change form, will be neither created nor destroyed during physical processes. If we construct a system, however, and some external force performs work on it, the result may be slightly different. If the work is positive, then the overall store of energy is increased; if it is negative, however, we can say that the overall energy of the system has decreased. Most of the time, physicists who notice that an external force is regularly influencing a system will simply enlarge the system to include the external force. Though there have been many cases in which physicists did not know what force was influencing an external object, there have never been any cases in which the law of conservation of energy has been found to be violated.

Linear momentum

In physics, linear momentum can be found by multiplying the mass and velocity of an object: $p = mv$, in which p is linear momentum. Momentum and velocity will always be in the same direction. Newton's second law describes momentum, stating that the rate of change of momentum is proportional to the force exerted, and is in the direction of the force. If we assume a closed and isolated system (that is, one in which no objects leave or enter, and upon which the sum of external forces is zero), then we can assume that the momentum of the system will neither increase nor decrease. That is, we will find that p is a constant. The law of conservation of linear momentum applies universally in physics, even in situations of extremely high velocity or subatomic particles.

Collisions

This concept of momentum takes on new importance when we consider collisions. Most people have a general idea of what the word collision means. In physics, however, the word has a more specialized meaning: it is an isolated event in which a relatively strong force acts on each of two or more colliding bodies for a relatively short period of time. In order for a collision to be subject to study, it must have a clear beginning, occurrence, and end. One of the most basic ways in which physicists conduct research is by causing a collision between two bodies, and investigating the changes that this collision produces.

When two bodies collide, we may call the equal but opposite forces that act upon them *F(t)* and *–F(t)*. These forces change the linear momentum of both of the objects. If we examine the change in linear momentum of each body involved in a collision, we will find that it is equal to the impulse acting on that body. This idea is known as the impulse-linear momentum theorem. Impulse and linear momentum are both vectors, and are expressed in the same units and dimensions. This theorem is a direct consequence of Newton's second law; it is not independent in any way. In other words, it means that energy is neither created nor destroyed by a collision. Let us imagine a situation in which a series of bodies with identical linear momenta collide with a fixed body. In each collision, the collision impulse on the fixed body will have the same magnitude, but the opposite direction, of the change in linear momenta experienced by the colliding bodies. If two bodies with identical mass and velocity are moving in opposite directions and collide with one another, they will simply stop. Otherwise, they will tend to move in the original direction of the larger or faster object, though at a reduced speed.

When discussing a collision in which one body is at rest before the collision, physicists will typically refer to the resting body as the target and the moving body as the projectile. If the system is closed, then the total amount of kinetic energy will remain the same and the collision will be elastic (that is, energy will be perfectly transferred). If the two bodies involved in an elastic collision have the same mass, then the body that was moving will stop completely, and the body that was at rest will begin moving at the same velocity as the projectile was moving before the collision. If one of the objects is much more massive than the other, one body bounces back in the opposite direction, and one continues on in the same direction.

During a collision, the center of mass of the system continues moving, unaffected by the violence of the collision. This is because the linear momentum of the system is unchanged by the collision. If the kinetic energy of a system of colliding bodies is conserved, the collision is considered inelastic. If the kinetic energy is completely transferred to other forms of energy, as for instance when a ball of putty hits the floor, it is called a completely inelastic collision. Considering, then, a system in which one body is initially stationary, we may say that the law of conservation of linear momentum will hold true. In inelastic collisions, the kinetic energy is usually converted into thermal energy.

Fluids

A few of the questions on the mechanical concepts portion of the MASS exam will probably require you to consider the behavior of fluids. It sounds obvious, perhaps, but fluids can best be defined as substances that flow. A fluid will conform, slowly or quickly, to any container in which it is placed. This is because a fluid is unable to maintain a force tangential to its surface. In other words, fluids cannot withstand shearing stress. They can, on the other hand, exert a force perpendicular to their surface. Both liquids and gases are considered to be fluids. Fluids, essentially, are those substances in which the atoms are not arranged in any permanent, rigid way. In ice, for instance, atoms are all lined up in what is known as a crystalline lattice, while in water and steam the only intermolecular arrangements are haphazard connections between neighboring molecules.

Density
The density of a fluid is generally expressed with the symbol ρ (the greek letter rho). In order to find the density of a particular fluid, we generally isolate a small volume of the fluid and determine its mass. Then, the density may be found with the simple equation: $\rho = \frac{\Delta m}{\Delta V}$. It is generally assumed that the volume will never be measured at an amount so small as to have an inordinate number of atoms, and so the density of the fluid will be the same everywhere. Density is a scalar property, meaning that it has no direction component; the density of a fluid is the same at every point in the fluid. While the density of a gas will tend to fluctuate considerably depending on the level of pressure, the density of a liquid is comparatively stable.

Pressure
In the case of fluids, pressure is typically measured by placing a small, spring-mounted sensor inside the fluid and measuring the degree to which the spring is compressed. Experiment has shown that the pressure will be the same no matter in which direction in the fluid the sensor is placed. Pressure, like fluid density, is a scalar, and does not have a direction. This is true even though the force compressing the spring of the sensor has a direction. The equation for pressure is concerned only with the magnitude of that force, not with the direction in which it is pointing. The SI unit of pressure is the Newton per square meter, or pascal.

As every deep-sea diver knows, the pressure of water becomes greater the deeper you go below the surface; conversely, experienced mountain climbers know that air pressure decreases as they gain a higher altitude. These pressures are typically referred to as hydrostatic pressures, because they involve fluids at rest. A mercury barometer is the most common way to measure the pressure of the atmosphere. It is constructed by filling a long glass tube with mercury and inverting it such that its open end is face-down in a dish of mercury. The top of the tube will contain mercury vapor, a fluid with an extremely low pressure. This instrument is then placed into the environment we seek to investigate, and we can look at the height attained by the mercury liquid to determine the pressure of the external environment.

Pascal's principle
The MASS exam may also require you to demonstrate some knowledge of how fluids move. Anytime you squeeze a tube of toothpaste, you are demonstrating the idea known as Pascal's principle. This principle states that a change in the pressure applied to an enclosed fluid is transmitted undiminished to every portion of the fluid as well as to the walls of the containing vessel. If, for instance, we had a container filled with liquid, on top of which a piston rests, loaded down with a lead weight. The atmosphere, container, lead weight, and piston will all be exerting pressure on the liquid. If we added another weight to the piston, however, we would be increasing pressure without in any way affecting the height of the liquid in the container. Since this is so, the pressure change will hold for all points within the liquid, as Pascal's principle suggests.

Buoyant force
If an object is submerged in water, it will have a buoyant force exerted on it in the upward direction. This force is caused by the difference in water pressure depending on depth: the object will naturally be propelled upward by the greater pressure at its bottom. Often, of course, this buoyant force is much too small to keep an object from sinking to the bottom. This buoyant force is one of

the reasons why it is easier to lift heavy objects when they are underwater. This idea of buoyancy is summarized in Archimedes' principle; a body wholly or partially submerged in a fluid will be buoyed up by a force equal to the weight of the fluid that the body displaces. A piece of wood floating on top of the water, for instance, will displace less water since it breaks the plane of the surface.

Even though the weight of a floating object is precisely balanced by a buoyant force, these forces will not necessarily act at the same point. The weight will act from the center of mass of the object, while the buoyancy will act from the center of mass of the hole in the water made by the object (known as the center of buoyancy). If the floating object is tilted, then the center of buoyancy will shift and the object may be unstable. In order to remain in equilibrium, the center of buoyancy must always shift in such a way that the buoyant force and weight provide a restoring torque, one that will restore the body to its upright position. This concept is of course crucial to the construction of boats which must always be made to encourage restoring torque.

Ideal fluids

Because the motion of actual fluids is extremely complex, the authors of the MASS exam usually refer to ideal fluids when they set up their problems. Using ideal fluids in fluid dynamics problems is a bit like discounting friction in other problems; it tends to make the process more comprehensible. Therefore, when we deal with ideal fluids, we are making four assumptions. It is important to keep these in mind when considering the behavior of fluids on the MASS exam. First, we are assuming that the flow is steady; in other words, the velocity of every part of the fluid is the same. We also assume that fluids are incompressible, and therefore have a consistent density. We assume that fluids are nonviscous, meaning that they flow easily and without resistance. Finally, we assume that the flow of ideal fluids is irrotational: that is, it particles in the fluid will not rotate around a center of mass.

Bernoulli's principle

When fluids move, they do not create or destroy energy; this modification of Newton's second law for fluid behavior is called Bernoulli's principle. It is essentially just a reformulation of the law of conservation of mechanical energy for fluid mechanics. One consequence of Bernoulli's equation is that if the elevation of the fluid remains constant, and the speed of a fluid particle increases as it travels along a streamline, the pressure will decrease. If the fluid slows down, the pressure will increase. So, the faster water spills over the top of the dam, the less pressure will be exerted against the dam wall.

There are a few common situations that demonstrate the relations asserted by Bernoulli's principle. For one thing, we might consider the case of a high wind blowing past a house. If the wind is strong enough, the pressure outside the window will be so much smaller than the pressure inside that the window will break outward. When hurricanes tear the flat roofs off of buildings, Bernoulli's principle is at work. Also, if we consider a case in which someone has punctured a hole in a tank of liquid, Bernoulli's principle declares that the velocity of the escaping water will be the same as if the water had been dropped from the top surface of the water to the point at which the hole was made.

A final example of Bernoulli's principle can be found in the airplane. Airplane wings are designed to take advantage of Bernoulli's principle so that an extremely heavy body can be lifted into the air. As the plane moves forward, air is forced down by the upward tilt of the wing, which is set at what is called the "attack angle." As the wing exerts a force on the airstream, so does the airstream push up on the wing, with a force that is called lift. Airplane wings are designed so that the streamlines will be wider below than above the wing, and so there is greater air pressure underneath the wing than above. This is consistent with the fact that there is an upward force acting on the wing. The speed of the air will be considerably smaller below the wing than above, as the air is deflected by the wing with a force known as induced drag.

Simple machines

This concludes our review of the basic physics concepts that may appear on the MASS exam. Obviously, individuals who are taking the MASS will not have to deal with all of these issues in a purely theoretical manner. For this reason, the MASS exam will focus on the ways that the basic properties of physics apply to mechanics. In order to understand how to make these applications, however, you will need to know the characteristics of the simple machines. Simple machines are the fundamental tools we use to make work easier. They include the inclined plane, the wedge, the screw, the pulley, the lever, and the wheel. Most of these machines are useful because they allow you to generate more force by increasing distance (remember the equation for work, *Work = force* x *distance*).

Mechanical advantage

The specific amount of benefit gained through the use of a machine is called the mechanical advantage. On some of the questions on the MASS exam, you will be asked to compare two or more simple machines to determine which makes a given task easier. In other words, you will be asked to find the mechanical advantage.

Inclined plane

The inclined plane is perhaps the most common of the simple machines. It is simply a flat surface that elevates as you move from one end to the other; a ramp is an easy example of an inclined plane. Consider how much easier it is for an elderly person to walk up a long ramp than to climb a shorter but steeper flight of stairs; this is because the force required is diminished as the distance increases. Indeed, the longer the ramp, the easier it is to ascend. On the MASS exam, this simple fact will most often be applied to moving heavy objects. For instance, if you have to move a heavy box onto the back of a truck, it is much easier to push it up a ramp than to lift it directly onto the truck bed. The longer the ramp, the greater the mechanical advantage, and the easier it will be to move the box. As you solve this kind of problem, however, remember that the same amount of work is being performed whether the box is lifted directly or pushed up a twenty-foot ramp; a simple machine only changes the force and the distance

Wedge

A wedge is a variation on the inclined plane, in which one focuses moreso on the disparity between the surface areas of the blade edge and flat edge than the slope of the plane itself. Perhaps the most familiar use of the wedge is in splitting wood. A wedge is driven into the wood by hitting the flat back end. The thin end of a wedge is easier to drive into the wood, because it has less surface area and therefore transmits more force per area. As the wedge is driven in, the increased width helps to split the wood. The MASS may require you to select the wedge that has the highest mechanical advantage. This should be easy: the longer and thinner the wedge, the greater the mechanical advantage. To put it into slightly more technical terms, the mechanical advantage of a wedge is determined by the ratio between the height and length of the wedge. Remember that wedges are not just used for splitting wood: knives, axes, and chisels also function as wedges. One unique characteristic of a wedge is that, unlike an inclined plane, it is designed to move.

Screw

A screw is simply an inclined plane that has been wound around a cylinder so that it forms a spiral. When it is placed into some medium, as for instance wood, the screw will move either forwards or backwards when it is rotated. The principle of the screw is used in a number of different objects, from jar lids to flashlights. On the MASS exam, you are unlikely to see many questions regarding screws, though you may be presented with a given screw rotation and asked in which direction the screw will move.

Lever

The lever is the most common kind of simple machine. See-saws, shovels, and baseball bats are all examples of levers. There are three classes of levers; they are differentiated by the relative orientations of the fulcrum, resistance, and effort. The fulcrum is the point at which the lever rotates; the effort is the point on the lever where force is applied; the resistance is the part of the lever that acts in response to the effort. In a first class lever, the fulcrum is between the effort and the resistance. A seesaw is a good example of a first class lever: when effort is applied to force one end up, the other end it goes down, and vice versa. The mechanical advantage created by a first class lever depends on the relative distance between the three components. The shorter the distance between the fulcrum and the resistance, the easier it will be to move the resistance. As an example, consider whether it is easier to lift another person on a see-saw when they are sitting close to the middle or all the way at the end. A little practice will show you that it is much more difficult to lift a person the farther away he or she is on the see-saw.

In a second class lever, the resistance is in between the fulcrum and the effort. Whereas a first class lever is able to increase force and distance through mechanical advantage, a second class lever is only able to increase force. A common example of a second class lever is the wrench: the force exerted by your hand at one end of the wrench is magnified at the other end. Basically, with a second class lever you are trading distance for force; by moving your end of the wrench a bit farther, you produce greater force at the other end.

Third class levers are used to produce greater distance. In a third class lever, the force is applied in between the fulcrum and the resistance. A baseball bat is a classic example of a third class lever; the bottom of the bat, below where you grip it, is considered the fulcrum. The end of the bat, where the ball is struck, is the resistance. By exerting effort at the base of the bat, close to the fulcrum, you are able to make the end of the bat fly quickly through the air, thus generating power. The closer your hands are to the base of the bat, the faster you will be able to make the other end of the bat travel.

Pulleys

The pulley is a simple machine in which a rope is carried by the rotation of a wheel. Another name for a pulley is a block. Pulleys are typically used to allow the force to be directed from a convenient location. For instance, imagine you are given the task of lifting a heavy and tall bookcase. Rather than tying a rope to the bookcase and trying to lift it up, it would make sense to tie a pulley system to a rafter above the bookcase and run the rope through it, so that you could pull down on the rope and lift the bookcase. Pulling down allows you to incorporate your weight (normal force) into the act of lifting, thereby making it easier.

If there is just one pulley above the bookcase, you have created a first-class lever which will not diminish the amount of force that needs to be applied to lift the bookcase. There is another way to use a pulley, however, that can make the job of lifting a heavy object considerably easier. First, tie the rope directly to the rafter. Then, attach a pulley to the top of the bookcase and run the rope through it. If you can then stand so that you are above the bookcase, you will have a much easier time lifting this heavy object. Why? Because the weight of the bookcase is now being distributed: half of it is acting on the rafter, and half of it is acting on you. In other words, this arrangement allows you to lift an object with half the force. This simple pulley system, therefore, has a mechanical advantage of 2. Note that in this arrangement, the unfixed pulley is acting like a second-class lever. The price you pay for your mechanical advantage is that whatever distance you raise your end of the rope, the bookcase will only be lifted half as much.

Of course, it might be difficult for you to find a place high enough to enact this system. If this is the case, you can always tie another pulley to the rafter and run the rope through it and back down to the floor. Since this second pulley is fixed, the mechanical advantage will remain the same.

There are other, slightly more complex ways to obtain an even greater mechanical advantage with a system of pulleys. All of these include one fixed pulley and one unfixed pulley, though the number of ropes running between these two pulleys may vary. On the MASS exam, you may be required to determine the pulley and tackle (rope) arrangement that creates the greatest mechanical advantage. The easiest way to determine the answer is to count the number of ropes that are going to and from the unfixed pulley; the more ropes coming and going, the greater the mechanical advantage.

Wheel and axle

Another basic arrangement that makes use of simple machines is called the wheel and axle. When most people think of a wheel and axle, they immediately envision an automobile tire. The steering wheel of the car, however, operates on the same mechanical principle, namely that the force required to move the center of a circle is much greater than the force require to move the outer rim of a circle. When you turn the steering wheel, you are essentially using a second-class lever. The force required to turn the wheel from the outer rim is much less than would be required to turn the wheel from its center. Just imagine how difficult it would be to drive a car if the steering wheel was the size of a saucer!

The MASS exam will not require you to calculate the mechanical advantage derived by a wheel and axle system with any degree of specificity, but you will need to understand some basic concepts of system function. For instance, all other things being equal, the mechanical advantage created by a system will increase along with the radius. In other words, a steering wheel with a radius of 12 inches has a greater mechanical advantage than a steering wheel with a radius of ten inches; the same amount of force exerted on the rim of each wheel will produce greater force at the axis of the larger wheel.

Gears

The MASS exam may ask you questions involving some slightly more complex mechanical contraptions. It is very common, for instance, for there to be a couple of questions concerning gears. Gears are a system of interlocking wheels that can create immense mechanical advantage. The amount of mechanical advantage, however, will depend on the gear ratio; that is, on the relation in size between the gears. When a small gear is driving a big gear, the speed of the big gear is relatively slow; when a big gear is driving a small gear, the speed of the small gear is relatively fast. This is the fundamental concept of gear ratio that you are likely to encounter on the MASS: the larger the driving gear in relation to the driven gear, the faster the driven gear will move. A common question format on the MASS presents a series of gear pairs and asks you to select the driven gear that will be moving the fastest. Always select the driven gear that is smallest in relation to its corresponding driving gear. When necessary, you can even calculate the gear ratio by comparing the number of teeth in the two gears. When the driving gear has 30 teeth and the driven gear has 10 teeth, the gear ratio is 3:1. You can calculate the respective gear ratios for a number of systems if you are unsure of which driven gear has the greatest speed. Naturally, this comparison only works when all of the driving gears are rotating with the same force.

Of course, remember that torque and speed are placed in an inverse relation to one another: when one goes up, the other goes down, and vice versa. Small gears always turn faster than large gears, but they produce less torque. Torque is a twisting force, like the force applied to a bolt with a wrench. Occasionally, a question on the MASS exam will ask you to indicate which driven gear is generating more torque. All other things being equal, the torque will increase in proportion to the size of the driven gear.

Two pulleys connected by a drive belt

A similar system involves two pulleys connected by a drive belt (a looped band that goes around both pulleys). The operation of this system is similar to that of gears, with the exception that the pulleys will rotate in the same direction, while interlocking gears will rotate in opposite directions. A smaller pulley will always spin faster than a larger pulley, though the larger pulley will generate more torque. The speed ratio between the pulleys can be determined by comparing their radii; for instance, a 12-inch pulley and a 4-inch pulley will have a speed ratio of 3:1.

This concludes an exhaustive review of all the content that may appear on the mechanical concepts section of the MASS exam. Hopefully, some of this material will be familiar to you from your high school physics or physical science class. If not, be sure to reread this section until you have a solid grasp on the important concepts. Try to imagine examples as you read, and take frequent breaks to let the ideas sink in. This is probably the most technical part of the MASS exam, but once you learn the basics of physics and mechanics, it will all seem like common sense.

Reading Comprehension

Every MASS examination will contain some reading comprehension questions. Although critical reading skills are not normally considered to be part of the repertoire of a power plant maintenance worker, in actuality you will be required to read and understand a number of different texts during the course of your service. For one thing, you will often have to engage in written correspondence with your employer or with your fellow employees. You need to be able to understand written directions and descriptions of equipment and operations. You will also have to stay abreast of the latest techniques and products available in your field, and for this you will need to be able to read and understand catalogs and training manuals. Finally, you may need to read local, state, and national regulations in order to avoid violating the law. The area in which you work may be heavily regulated by the government, and so it is no exaggeration to say that your livelihood and the livelihood of your employer may depend on your ability to understand that which you read.

With this in mind, let's take a look at the reading comprehension questions that will appear on the MASS exam. As mentioned above, the reading comprehension section will include 32 multiple-choice questions that must be completed within 30 minutes. These questions will be based on four passages of several paragraphs each. These passages will pertain to topics related to energy, power plants, and other subjects related to the field of plant maintenance. However, you will not be required to have any special knowledge to answer the reading comprehension questions. In fact, the directions in this section will specifically warn you to base your answers solely on the information found within the passage; in other words, do not base your answers on your own experience or knowledge of a particular subject.

It is important, then, to remember the purpose of the reading comprehension questions is to test your reading ability, and not to assess your knowledge of the topic. The reading comprehension exercises on the exam are designed to assess your ability to read carefully, analyze the relationships among different parts of a passage, and draw inferences from the material in the passage. The reading comprehension questions on the exam are of four basic types (main idea, detail, tone, and extending the author's reasoning), each of which calls for a slightly different approach.

The format of reading comprehension questions should not pose any problems. Each of the four passages will be followed by eight questions. These questions will be in a multiple-choice format, with four or five possible correct answers. For the most part, questions pertaining to the beginning of the passage will come before questions pertaining to the end of the passage. The reading comprehension questions on the exam are meant to be comprehensible to a general audience, and will not contain any specialized jargon. Also, all of the information required to answer the questions will be found in the passages; you will not need any outside information or experience. Now, let's take a quick look at the content of the passages that will appear on the exam.

The reading comprehension passages on MASS exams all pertain to subjects related to energy, electricity, and power plants, though they may come from a number of different genres. At least one of the passages will be an excerpt from a training manual of some kind. This passage will feature clear, technical language and a strict attention to organization. Training manuals outline the steps in a process and tend to proceed in a clear and orderly fashion. Other passages will be written in a legal style, and will pertain to building regulations or codes. These passages will be dense and full of information; you are likely to be asked to recall specific details. When you are confronted with an extremely technical passage, do not feel that you have to memorize all of the details. Simply remember where the information is located in the passage so that you can refer back to it in the future. A final type of passage will be a biographical account of some famous inventor or tradesman. These passages are designed to be entertaining as well as informative, and will likely include colorful descriptions and interesting anecdotes. When you are presented with a passage of this type, it is likely that you will be asked to describe the author's attitude towards his or her subject.

Now that we have covered the content areas from which the reading comprehension passages will be drawn, let us consider the types of questions that you will encounter. The first and most basic kind of reading comprehension question is the one that asks you to define the main idea of the passage. This question may arrive in any of a few different forms. The question may ask you for the "the best summary," the "salient point," or the "overarching theme" of the passage. Do not be confused by the precise language: this is a main idea question. As you no doubt have learned by now, the main idea of a passage is most likely to appear in either the first or the last sentence. Therefore, as you are reading a passage for the first time, pay special attention to the beginning and end. Whether the main idea is offered first or last will depend on the type of passage: expository passages tend to give a main idea first and then spend the rest of the sentences defending it, while critical or argumentative essays will often begin with a set of loose facts and end with a summarizing conclusion. In any case, be prepared to refer back to the text in search of the main idea.

On occasion, the authors of the exam will try to fool you by asking you to provide the main idea of a specific *part* of the passage rather than of the passage as a whole. Similarly, they may try to confuse you with answer choices that are true without being the main idea of the passage. For this reason, it is imperative that you read the question carefully and do not just assume that the first or last sentence of the paragraph is the main idea. The main idea is not just any true statement contained within the passage: it is the idea that most effectively summarizes the entire passage.

It is certain that at least a couple of the reading comprehension questions will ask you to determine the main idea. In addition, it is quite likely that a few of the questions will ask you to recall specific details from the passage. This would appear to be the easiest kind of question to answer, but many students go astray by relying on memory instead of scrolling back up to find the pertinent details in the passage. Remember that you are free to refer to the text as much as you like. Also, remember that specific questions are likely to have specific answers, just as general questions are likely to have general answers. In other words, if the question asks you to name a concept, the answer probably will not be a piece of specific data.

A more subtle form of question is the one that requires you to diagnose the author's attitude. As with the main idea question, this kind of question can take a number of different forms. It may ask you to describe the "tone," "opinion," "feeling" or "mood" of the author or passage. All of these questions are essentially asking you to assess how the author feels about his or her topic. In order to answer such a question, you will have to pay attention to the specific language used by the author, and the point of view that the language conveys. For instance, if the author is describing a small person, he or she would create a sharply different tone by using the word *puny* than by using the word *petite. Puny* suggests a shriveled, scrawny individual, while *petite* conjures daintiness and delicacy. It may take a little bit of practice before you habitually notice these shades of meaning, but you should try to be conscious of the ways in which language can be used to subtly indicate attitude. For the most part, the test administrators avoid passages that are violently opinionated or controversial. Any answer choices that suggest the author holds an opinion which could be considered radical or offensive are most likely incorrect.

The final category of question which you may encounter on the exam is one that asks you to extend the author's reasoning. Put another way, these questions require you to consider the information provided in the passage and then use this information to consider a problem not mentioned in the passage. For example, a passage might describe the characteristics of a given community and the police activity that is recommended for that community. A question might then ask you to extend the reasoning of the author by describing the changes in police activity that could be made in response to a change in the community. The reasoning required to answer these kinds of questions will not be extremely complicated. The most common problem students have with questions asking them to extend the reasoning of the passage is that they attempt to find the answer explicitly in the passage. Remember that even though all of the information needed to answer every question can be found in the text, some questions will require you to do some independent thinking.

The best way to prepare for the reading comprehension section of the written examination is to practice reading a variety of different texts. By visiting the local library, you should be able to obtain journal articles, training manuals, and general interest articles on issues related to power plant maintenance. As you read these texts, practice finding the main idea and identifying key details. You may want to practice scanning a short passage to determine the basic structure, before you go back and read in more detail. You will be allowed to make notes and underline on the written examination, so feel free to do this during your practice if it helps you to understand the text.

Mathematical Usage

Those individuals hoping to avoid dealing with math by becoming a power plant maintenance worker will be disappointed when they sit for the MASS examination. Power plant maintenance workers are required to use basic math skills every day, and so it is important for you to demonstrate a solid foundation of knowledge in this section of the test. The mathematical usage section of the MASS consists of 18 questions, to be completed within seven minutes. These questions primarily pertain to arithmetic, though there may be some questions which require knowledge of basic algebra and geometry. The level of difficulty is approximately that of a sophomore- or junior-year math class in high school. So, with a little bit of a refresher, you should have no problem with this section of the exam.

The format of the mathematical usage questions should be familiar to you from other standardized tests. You will be asked to solve a problem, find the value of a variable, or provide some other piece of information. Many of the mathematical usage questions will be word problems, in which you are asked to make a calculation based on the information given in a short passage. We will look at a couple of sample word problems a little later in this section.

Mathematical usage questions are in a multiple-choice format, with either four or five possible answers from which to choose. When these answer choices are real numbers without variables, they will usually be listed in order from least to greatest. One exception to this rule is when a question concerns the relative value of the answer choices. For instance, in a question asking you to select the greatest of a group of fractions, the answer choices will be listed in a random order.

Some of the mathematical usage questions will include graphs, charts, or geometric figures. Unless the exam specifies so, these drawings will not be perfectly accurate and to scale. You should never make any assumptions about a diagram on the exam; only consider information that is either explicitly given by the question or that can be calculated based on information explicitly given.

The most important thing to remember regarding mathematical usage questions is to read the question carefully and make sure you understand what it is asking. For instance, the exam is notorious for setting up an equation like $2x = 6$ and then asking you to solve for $x + 2$. Inevitably, many test takers will see the equation and simply solve for x; thus the exam punishes those who fail to read the question carefully. Therefore, before you even begin to solve the problem or examine the answer choices, make sure you know what the directions are asking you to do.

On many of the mathematical usage questions, the exam will not require the highest level of specificity. For instance, when the answer to a problem is a decimal with nine places, the answer choices will often round to the nearest hundredth or thousandth. Before you go to the trouble of working out the problem to the millionths place, take a look at the answer choices: you may be able to save yourself some labor.

Although calculators are not allowed on the exam, scratch paper and pencils will be made available. You should use this scratch paper as much as you can. Do not try to solve complicated problems in your head; put them down on paper so that you can get a visual sense and leave your mind free to work. The importance of scratch paper is true for the data sufficiency questions as well as the mathematical usage questions, but on the mathematical usage questions you should use the paper to solve each problem forwards and backwards. For instance, on a question that asks you to solve for a specific variable, you should solve for the variable, then plug that variable back into the original equation and make sure that it works. After you have reviewed basic arithmetic and algebra, you should have plenty of time to work out problems forwards and backwards on your scratch paper. By double checking your work in this way, you can prevent careless mistakes from lowering your score.

Let's consider an example of working backwards to solve a tricky mathematical usage question. Imagine that you are given the following scenario:

> *Brian takes an 81-inch piece of rope and cuts it three times. Each time he cuts the rope, he cuts off and discards the same fraction of the remaining length. When he is finished, the piece of rope is 3 inches long. Which fraction represents the amount of rope removed in each of the three cuts?*

This is a difficult question, and you may not know exactly how to approach it. This is when working backwards from the given answer choices can be an effective strategy. Let us imagine that the five answer choices for this problem are 1/8, 1/3, ½, 2/3, and ¾. When the answer choices are grouped in ascending order like this, it is a good idea to start with the middle value; if this answer is incorrect, you can often tell whether the right answer will be higher or lower.

So, returning to our example, let us begin with ½. If this is the correct answer, then the 3-inch rope left at the end of the problem would have been half the size of the rope remaining after two cuts. So, the amount of rope remaining after two cuts would be 6 inches. We can proceed on in this way: after one cut, the length of the rope would be 12 inches; before any cuts have been made, then, the length of the rope would be 24 inches. Obviously, since we know that the original length of the rope was 81 inches, ½ cannot be the correct answer. Furthermore, since plugging ½ into the problem yields an answer significantly smaller than we require, we can guess that the correct answer will be greater than ½.

Let us next consider 2/3, then. Remember that if 2/3 of the rope is cut off each time, the remaining amount will be 1/3 of the length before the cut. So, if the amount left after the third cut (3 inches) is 1/3 of the length of the rope before the third cut, the length of the rope before the third cut must be 9 inches (3 x 3 = 9). We can thus determine the preceding lengths of rope by multiplying by 3: before the second cut the length would have been 27 inches, and before the first cut, 81 inches. Aha! We can now be sure that 2/3 is the correct answer to the problem. Furthermore, we discovered this simply by working backwards from the answer choices given by the test.

There are some mathematical usage questions, however, for which it is not prudent to work both forwards and backwards. This is true of problems in which working backwards would require too much time and effort. On these problems, it may be more efficient to set up a basic algebraic equation to derive the information you need. For instance, consider the following problem:

> *Vincenzo's Gourmet Coffee sells medium roast beans for $7 a pound and dark roast beans for $6 a pound. If Denise orders a 12-pound mixture that costs $6.25 per pound, how many pounds of dark roast beans is she getting?*

The answer choices for this problem are 3, 6, 8, 9, and 10. Certainly, it would be possible to solve this problem by working backward. If you chose 8 as your starting point, you could multiply by 6 and add the product (48) to the product of the amount of medium roast beans and their cost per pound ($4 \times 7 = 28$). You could then add these two products together and divide by 12 to determine the cost per pound of Denise's mixture: $(48 + 28)/12 = \$6.33$. This is the wrong answer.

Obviously, you would have to go to a fair amount of trouble to calculate the answer this way. For this reason, it is better to set up an algebraic equation using the information given in the problem. The variable x will represent the number of dark roast beans in the mixture. The amount of medium roast beans can therefore be represented as $12 - x$. We know that the total cost of the dark roast beans in the mixture, $6x$, added to the total cost of the medium roast beans in the mixture, $7(12 - x)$, can be divided by the number of pounds of the mixture, 12, to yield the cost per pound, which we know to be $6.25. In other words, we can set up the following equation to find the number of pounds of dark roast beans in the mixture: $[6x + 7(12 - x)]/ 12 = 6.25$. Multiply both sides by 12, and then multiply the 7 across the parentheses, yielding: $6x + 84 - 7x = 75$. Simplify and subtract 84 from both sides, to obtain: $-x = -9$. Make both sides of the equation positive, to obtain: $x = 9$. Of course, developing and solving this equation has its perils, but it is far less time-consuming and less liable to careless error than working backward through a long series of calculations.

Finally, a few of the mathematical usage questions on your exam will include geometric figures. Some geometry-style problems will not be accompanied by a figure, and it will be in your best interest to draw one of your own on scratch paper. In either case, remember that you can only trust information about the figure that is explicitly given. The exam will usually try to draw figures to scale, but it does not always succeed, and therefore never make any assumptions about the relative sizes or angles of a figure. That being said, you can often derive some useful extra information from the values in the figures that are given. For instance, if you are given a square and told that one side is 6 inches long, you automatically know that all four sides are 6 inches long. Furthermore, you will know that every angle of the square is 90 degrees. This information may be required to find the answer to the problem.

The mathematical usage section of the exam is broken down into three main content areas: arithmetic, algebra, geometry. The vast majority of the mathematics questions will require you to perform basic calculations with whole numbers, fractions, and decimals. As mentioned earlier, the level of difficulty of this section of the exam should not exceed an eleventh-grade level. Following is an outline of all the specific topics included in the exam. (Note: Do not try to read this section at once! Either work through it paragraph by paragraph, or use it as a reference for those topics that are unfamiliar or rusty. Space constraints prevent us from describing every topic exhaustively, so you may need to seek outside assistance on especially troublesome topics.)

Integers

Quite a few of the questions on the exam will require you to understand some of the basic properties of numbers, specifically integers. The set of numbers known as integers is composed of all the so-called counting numbers, both negative and positive, and including zero. So, expressed as a mathematical set, integers are {...-3, -2, -1, 0, 1, 2, 3...}. Fractions and decimals are not integers. Any integer that is a multiple of two is called an even integer; all other integers are considered to be odd. Zero is considered to be an even integer. Zero has some special properties: any number multiplied by zero will yield a product of zero, and it is not possible to divide a number by zero. Any groups of integers that are arranged in order from least to greatest, and without any gaps, are referred to as consecutive integers.

Place value

The value of an integer depends not only on the identity of the digits but on their placement. For instance, the numbers 0.61 and 0.061 are not the same. The position of a digit in a number is referred to as its place value. In order to answer some of the questions on the exam, you may need to be familiar with the more common place values. In a number that does not have a decimal point, the names of the place value increase by powers of ten as you move to the left. For instance, in the number 56,324, four is in the ones place, two is in the tens place, three is in the hundreds place, six is in the thousands place, and five is in the ten thousands place. It is easy to imagine how the progression of increasing places will continue: hundred thousands, millions, ten millions, etc. The place values on the right side of the decimal point also progress by powers of ten, beginning with tenths. As an example, in the number 0.5297, five is in the tenths place, two is in the hundredths place, nine is in the thousandths place, and seven is in the ten thousandths place. Again, it easy to imagine how these decreasing places will continue: hundred thousandths, millionths, ten millionths. Note that all of the place values to the right of the decimal point have a "th" at the end; make sure you don't confuse the thousands and the thousandths place on your exam.

Prime and composite numbers

Any number that can only be divided evenly by itself or one is a prime number. For example, three is a prime number because it can only be divided by three and one; four is not a prime number because it can be divided by two as well as by four and one. All numbers that are not prime numbers are referred to as composite numbers. Prime numbers are always positive, always whole numbers, and almost always odd (2 is the only even prime number).

Operations with integers

Arithmetic is basically just performing operations with integers. There are a few things to remember when working with negative integers. A good rule of thumb is to remember that two negatives equal a positive: subtracting a negative number is the same as adding it; multiplying or dividing two negative numbers yields a positive product or quotient. On the other hand, when only one of the terms in a multiplication or division product is negative, the resulting product or quotient will be negative as well. When one integer cannot be divided evenly into another, the number that is left over is called the remainder. For example, in the problem 5 ÷ 2, two can go into five two times, with a remainder of one; this is expressed 2 r 1.

Factors and multiples

For any integer, the set of numbers which can be divided into that integer is known as its set of factors. Prime numbers will only have two factors: themselves and one. Composite number will have at least three factors: themselves, one, and some other number. The number 8, for example, has four factors: 8, 4, 2, and 1.

The multiples of an integer are all of the values produced when the integer is multiplied by another integer. The multiples of 3 are 3, 6, 9, 12, and so on. The multiples of 4 are 4, 8, 12, 16, 20, and so on.

Associative and distributive properties

There are a few basic arithmetic properties which, although they are unlikely to be specifically mentioned on the exam, may help you to figure out some other problems. The associative property of addition asserts that the order of the terms in an addition problem does not matter, and so the various terms can be grouped and organized in any way without affecting the total. As an example, (2 + 5) + 6 = 13; and 2 + (5 + 6) = 13. Also, for that matter, 2 + 6 + 5 = 13, and 5 + 6 + 2 = 13. As long as the terms in an addition problem do not change, the sum will not change either.

In a similar vein, the associative property of multiplication asserts that the grouping of the terms in a multiplication problem will not affect the product. So, for example, 5 (2 x 3) = 30, 3 (2 x 5) = 30, 3 x 2 x 5 = 30, 5 x 2 x 3 = 30, and so on.

The distributive law is only slightly more complicated. It states that any number multiplied by a set of values within parentheses is multiplied by every value within the parentheses. To illustrate, 3 (5 + 4) = 3(5) + 3(4). Occasionally, the exam will ask you to transform a problem in the opposite way, as follows: 3(17) + 3 (14) = 3 (17 + 14). The problem may even be written in a slightly more confusing manner, such as: 5(12) - 83(5) = 5 (12 - 83).

Absolute value

The absolute value of a number is its distance from zero. Absolute value is denoted by two vertical lines. Since absolute value is the measure of distance, it cannot be negative. So, the absolute value of 6, written |6|, is 6, and the absolute value of -6 is 6 as well.

Fractions

A fraction, for instance ½, consists of a numerator on top and a denominator on the bottom. Fractions are said to be equivalent when they can be reduced to be the same thing; for example, 5/10 is equivalent to ½, because it can be reduced to ½ by dividing both numerator and denominator by 5. Remember that when reducing a fraction you must divide numerator and denominator by the same number. In order to perform addition or subtraction operations with fractions, you must have a common denominator. Once you have a common denominator, you simply perform the operation with the numerators, leaving the denominators alone. To multiply two fractions, multiply the numerators together and then multiply the denominators together. To divide one fraction by another, invert the second fraction and then multiply first numerators and then denominators. A fraction in which the numerator is greater than the denominator is called an improper fraction. An expression consisting of a whole number and a fraction—for instance 5 ½—is called a mixed number.

Decimals

Decimals, like fractions, are a way of expressing values other than integers. Indeed, every fraction has an equivalent decimal: for instance, the fraction ¼ is equivalent to the decimal 0.25. When working with decimals, it is very important to understand how different operations affect the number of places to the right of the decimal point. When adding or subtracting decimals, the resulting sum or difference should have as many decimal places as the term in the operation with the most decimal places. In the problem 1.5 + 1.05, for example, the answer must have two numbers to the right of the decimal point. One way to simplify such problems is to add zeroes to the ends of those numbers with fewer decimal places; for instance, making our example 1.50 + 1.05. When two decimals are multiplied together, the resulting product will have the sum of the decimal places in the two terms. In other words, the product of 3.55 x 4.785 will have five places to the right of the decimal point, because the first term has two and the second term has three. In order to divide decimals, the divisor must be converted into an integer by moving the decimal point to the right. So, in order to complete the problem 5.55 ÷ 2.8, we would need to shift the decimal point in both terms one place to the right, resulting in the problem 55.5 ÷ 28. The resulting quotient will have one place to the right of the decimal point.

Exponents

When the number is multiplied by itself several times, we use a form of notation called an exponent. For instance, the number 2^5 is expressed verbally as "two to the fifth power," and is equivalent to 2 x 2 x 2 x 2 x 2. When a number is raised to the second power (that is, when its exponent is 2), we say that the number is being "squared." When a number is raised to the third power (exponent is 3), we say that the number is being "cubed." For any number, an exponent of zero makes the number equal to 1. When the number has a negative exponent, is equal to one over the number raised to the absolute value of the exponent; in other words, $x^{-1} = 1/x$; $x^{-2} = 1/x^2$; $x^{-3} = 1/x^3$.

Operations with exponents

There are specific rules for multiplying and dividing numbers with exponents. When two terms with the same base are multiplied together, as for example 2^3 x 2^4, the exponents are added together: 2^3 x $2^4 = 2^7$. When two terms with different bases but the same exponent are multiplied together, as in 2^3 x 3^3, only the two bases are multiplied: 2^3 x $3^3 = 6^3$. When the same base is given two exponents, as in $(3^2)^3$, the exponents are multiplied together: $(3^2)^3 = 3^6$. When two terms with the same base but different exponents are involved in a division problem, as in $3^4/3^2$, the exponent in the denominator is subtracted from the exponent in the numerator: $3^4/3^2 = 3^2$. Finally, when a fraction is given an exponent, as in $(3/4)^2$, the exponent applies to both the numerator and the denominator: $(3/4)^2 = 3^2/4^2$.

Square roots

The number that when multiplied by itself would produce a given number is called the "square root" of that given number; for instance, 2 is the square root of 4, since 2 x 2 = 4. Note that -2 could also be considered a square root of 4, since -2 x -2 = 4. Every positive number will have two square roots, one of which will be negative. Also, because any positive or negative number multiplied by itself has a positive product, negative numbers do not have square roots. (This will probably not come up on the exam, but the square root of 0 is 0, because $0^2 = 0$). The standard notation for, say, the square root of two, is $\sqrt{2}$. If a question is specifically asking for the negative square root of 2, this is expressed $-\sqrt{2}$. When two square roots are multiplied together, the numbers are simply multiplied and the resulting product remains as a square root: $\sqrt{2} \times \sqrt{3} = \sqrt{6}$. In like fashion, when one square root is divided by another, the terms inside the root symbol are divided and the square root sign is left intact: $\sqrt{8}/\sqrt{4} = \sqrt{2}$.

Order of operations

There is a specific order in which the various components of an arithmetic problem must be performed. This system is known as the order of operations, and is as follows: parentheses, exponents, multiplication, division, addition, and subtraction. The order of operations is easy to follow if you just remember the mnemonic phrase "Please excuse my dear Aunt Sally." The first letters of the words in this sentence (Please Excuse My Dear Aunt Sally) mirror those of the order of operations: Parentheses, Exponents, Multiplication, Division, Addition, and Subtraction. So, as an example, take a look at the following arithmetic expression: $3(4 + 3^2) - 2$. In order to derive the correct answer, you would need to begin by determining the value of the parentheses, first by calculating the exponent 3^2, and then by adding 4. Next, you would multiply by 3 (because multiplication preceded subtraction in the order of operations), and finally you would subtract 2. The correct value of this expression is 37. Note that if you tried to calculate the value of this expression without observing the proper order of operations (say, by subtracting 2 from the parentheses before multiplying by 3) you would not find the same answer.

Percents

When a number is expressed as a percentage, this means that it is being expressed as a portion of 100. So, 25% is equivalent to 25 hundredths, or 0.25. Another way to express this is as a fraction: 25/100. If you prefer, you can always convert the percentages on the exam into decimals or fractions. The most common kind of percentage problem you will see on the exam is one that asks you to find a certain percentage of the given number. These problems are easily solved by multiplying the decimal equivalent of the percentage by the given number. As an example, imagine you are asked to calculate 25% of 40; you would simply multiply 0.25 by 40, resulting in an answer of 10 (remember the rules for multiplying decimals!). A similar kind of question will ask you to determine what percentage of a given number another number is. For instance, a question might ask what percentage of 40 the number 8 is. The way to solve this kind of problem is to set up a proportional equation as follows: $8/40 = x/100$. This equation can be expressed as "8 is to 40 as *x* is to 100." Such an equation can then be solved by cross multiplying and solving for *x*, yielding an answer of 20%.

Ratios

Another name for the proportion on either side of the last percentage equation is ratio. A ratio is simply a comparison between numbers. Indeed, ratios are noted in the same way as verbal analogies, as both involve a consideration of the relationship between two things. The ratio 4 to 5, then, would be expressed 4:5. Ratios can also be expressed as fractions: for example, 4/5. Some ratios can be simplified. For instance, in the ratio 8:12, both terms are divisible by 4, so we can simplify the ratio to 2:3.

Lines and angles

The basic unit of geometry is the line. Unless it is specified otherwise, lines are assumed to travel in opposite directions infinitely. Lines that are finite are called line segments. Where two lines intersect, angles are formed. The exam will require you to know a few of the basic types of angles. A right angle is one in which the two sides of the angle are perpendicular to one another; a right angle measures 90°. An acute angle has a measure between 0° and 90°. An obtuse angle has a measure between 90° and 180°. An angle with a measure of 180° is called a straight angle, although for all intents and purposes this is just a straight line. Two or more angles that add up to 90° are referred to as complementary angles. Two or more angles that add up to 180° are referred to as supplementary angles. There is no such thing as a negative angle, or an angle measuring 0°. When two lines intersect and form 4 angles, the angles opposite one another are referred to as vertical angles; vertical angles are always equal. When two parallel lines (i.e., lines extending infinitely in either direction but never touching) are intersected by a third line, known as a transversal, the corresponding angles formed are called transverse angles.

Triangles

There are a few properties and varieties of triangles that you will need to know for the exam. In every triangle, the largest angle is opposite the longest side. The sum of the lengths of the two smallest sides of a triangle will be greater than the length of the longest side. When the measures of the angles inside a triangle are added up, the sum is always 180°. A triangle with three equal sides into three equal angles is known as an equilateral triangle. A triangle with two equal angles and two equal sides is referred to as an isosceles triangle. A triangle that has no equal sides and no equal angles is referred to as a scalene triangle. Any triangle in which one angle is equal to 90° is called a right triangle. In such a triangle, the two sides that form the right angle are called the legs, and the other side is called the hypotenuse. The Pythagorean theorem describes one unique property of right triangles: the sum of the squares of the lengths of the two legs is equal to the length of the hypotenuse squared. This is usually written as: $a^2 + b^2 = c^2$. Remember that the Pythagorean theorem only works for right triangles.

Quadrilaterals and other polygons

A quadrilateral is any figure with four sides, in which the four interior angles add up to 360°. There are a few special quadrilaterals. A quadrilateral with four equal sides and four right angles is called a square. A quadrilateral with four equal sides and four interior angles that are not equal is called a rhombus. A quadrilateral with four equal angles and two opposite and equal pairs of sides is called a rectangle. All the angles in a rectangle are right angles. A quadrilateral with two opposite and equal pairs of sides and two opposite and equal pairs of non-right angles is called a parallelogram. A quadrilateral with four unequal angles and one pair of parallel sides is called a trapezoid.

Triangles and quadrilaterals are the types of polygons (closed figures) you are most likely to encounter on the exam. You should know the names of some other regular polygons, however. A regular polygon is one in which all the sides and all the angles are equal. A regular polygon with five sides is called a pentagon, one with six sides is called a hexagon, one with seven sides is called a heptagon, one with eight sides is called an octagon, one with nine sides is called a nonagon and one with ten sides is called a decagon. There is a simple formula for determining the sum of the interior angles in a regular polygon: simply subtract two from the number of sides and multiply by 180°; this is most often written as: *(n-2)180°* The sum of the interior angles of a pentagon, for instance, would be (5 – 2) 180° = 540°. You can find the measure of each interior angle by dividing the sum of the interior angles by the number of sides in the figure: 540°/5 = 108°.

Circles

In geometry, a circle is defined as all of the points in a plane that are the same distance from a given point (the center of the circle). The distance from the center of a circle to any point on its border is known as the radius. Any line that passes from one edge of the circle to another is called a chord. The length of a line extending from one edge of the circle to another and passing through the center is known as the diameter. The diameter is the longest chord in any given circle. The diameter of a circle is twice the radius. The distance around the edge of the circle is known as the circumference of the circle. The circumference of a circle can be determined with the following equation: $c = 2\pi r$, in which r is the radius of the circle. The set of points including and connecting any two points on the edge of the circle is called an arc of the circle. Like angles, arcs are measured in degrees; the largest possible arc is 360°. Any line that intersects with a circle in exactly one point is called a tangent of that circle, and the line itself is considered tangent *to* the circle. The radius running from the center of the circle to the point at which a tangent intersects the edge of the circle will be perpendicular to the tangent. Two or more circles that share a center but have different diameters are referred to as concentric circles.

Area and perimeter

You will need to know a few basic formulae for calculating the area of various figures. The area of the triangle is calculated: $a = \frac{1}{2}(base \times height)$, where the base is one side of the triangle and the height runs perpendicular to the base. The perimeter of the triangle, and indeed the perimeter of any polygon, is the sum of the lengths of the sides. The area of a square, rectangle, or parallelogram can be calculated by multiplying the length by the width. The area of a rhombus can be calculated by multiplying one half by the product of the two diagonals (lines drawn between the vertices of opposing angles). The area of a circle is found: $a = \pi r^2$, in which r is the radius of the circle.

Cylinders, rectangular solids, and cubes

Occasionally, the exam will require you to work with basic three-dimensional figures like cubes, cylinders, and rectangular solids. A cylinder (shaped like a can) has two parallel circular bases of equal diameter. The height of a cylinder is measured perpendicular to the bases. The surface area of a cylinder is measured with the equation $A = 2(\pi r^2) + 2\pi rh$, in which r is the radius of the bases and h is the height. The volume of a cylinder can be calculated with the equation $V = \pi r^2 h$. A rectangular solid (shaped like a box) has six faces and twelve edges, connected at eight vertices. The volume of a rectangular solid is calculated with the equation $V = lwh$, in which l is length, w is width, and h is height. If these three measures are equal, the rectangular sold is called a cube. The surface area of a rectangular solid is calculated with the equation $A = 2(wl + lh + wh)$; in other words, surface area is the sum of the areas of the six faces of the rectangular solid.

Mean, median, mode

Some questions on the exam may present you with a set of data and ask you to name the mean, median, or mode of the set. The mean of a set is the same thing as the average, and is calculated in the same way, namely by adding together all the values in the set and dividing by the number of values in the set. For instance, then, in the set of data {5, 6, 4, 9}, the mean would be calculated as follows: (5 + 6 + 4 + 9)/ 4 = 6. The median of a set is the middle value when the set is arranged from least to greatest. Therefore, in the set {1, 3, 5}, the median is 3. If the set contains an even number of values, the median is calculated by adding together the 2 middle values and dividing by 2. So, for the set {2, 4, 6, 8}, the median would be calculated: (4 + 6)/2 = 5. Finally, the mode of a set of data is the value within the set that occurs most frequently. Sometimes, a set will have more than one mode, or, if every value within the set appears only once, it will not really have a mode at all.

Range and standard deviation

For any given set of values, the range is the distance from the greatest value to the least. This can be calculated by subtracting the least value from the greatest. So, for the set {2, 5, 7, 8, 12), the range would be calculated 12 – 2 = 10. The method of calculating range is not affected by the number of values in the set, or by the number of values that share the least or greatest measure.

Calculating the range is a rather crude way of judging the dispersion of values in a set of data. A more sophisticated measure is standard deviation. The process of determining standard deviation has several steps. First, the arithmetic mean of the set must be calculated. Next, the difference between each member of the set and the arithmetic mean must be found, and these differences must be squared and added together. This sum is then divided by the number of values in the set, and the square root of the quotient is found. This is defined by the formula:

$$\sigma = \sqrt{\frac{\left(\sum_{i=1}^{N}(x_i - \mu)^2\right)}{N}}$$

where σ (sigma) is the standard deviation, x_i is the particular value in question, μ (mu) is the average of the set of values and N is the total number of values in the set. One thus sees that the standard deviation is the absolute value of this square root (because standard deviation cannot be negative). Although it is unlikely that you will be required to calculate the standard deviation for a set of data, you should still have a working knowledge of the method for calculating standard deviation. It is more typical for a question to give you the mean and the standard deviation of a set, and then to ask you to determine the range of a certain number of standard deviations from the mean. For example, say a set of data has a mean of 6 and a standard deviation of 2. If you are asked to calculate the range of values within 2 standard deviations of the mean, you can do so by first multiplying the standard deviation by 2. Standard deviation extends to either side of the arithmetic mean, so the range will be all the values within 4 on either side of the mean. In other words, the range of values within 2 standard deviations of 6 will be 2 through 10.

Average

The word *average* is synonymous with the word *median*. The basic rule for finding the average of a set of data is to add up all the members of the set and then divide by the number of members. The average of a set containing 1, 3, 6, and 6 would be calculated: $(1 + 3 + 6 + 6)/4 = 4$.

Some problems will give you the average of an incomplete set of data and ask you to identify the missing term. You can solve this kind of problem by rearranging the equation for finding an average. Instead of average = sum/# of members, use sum = average x # of members. So for instance, if you are told that the average of a set containing 7, 5, x, and 20 is 10, you can determine that the sum of the members of the set must be $10 \times 4 = 40$. Since the known members of the set add up to 32, the missing member of the set must be 8.

On rare occasions, you may have to deal with weighted averages, in which some of the values in the set are given more importance than others. For example, imagine that during the last ten games a certain baseball team scored 8 runs one time, 4 runs three times, 2 runs five times, and 0 runs one time. You could not simply add up 8, 4, 2, and 0 and divide by 4 to find the average number of runs scored over the last ten games. Instead, you need to set the number of members of the set as ten, and then multiply each value by its number of occurrences before adding. Therefore the average would be calculated as follows: $[1(8) + 3(4) + 5(2) + 1(0)]/10 = 3$.

Distance, rate, and time

Probably the most common type of word problem on the exam is the one that asks you to consider distance, rate, and time. You will recognize these problems; they begin with something like, "John drives 3 hours at 50 miles per hour. How many miles does John drive?" In other words, two values are given and you are asked to find the third. This is easy enough when you remember the simple equation *distance* = *rate* x *time*. In the example problem, the rate is 50 mph and the time is 3 hours, ergo the distance is 150 miles. Always make sure that the units in the problem are consistent, as you will not get very far trying to convert kilometers per hour into miles. Also, be aware that the unknown variable will not always be distance, in which case you will need to rearrange the equation to solve for rate or time. For instance, if the problem states that "Dale drives 75 miles at 25 miles per hour," and asks you to determine how many hours Dale has been driving, you will need to solve for t, and thus your equation will be $t = d/r$. If the problem asks you to solve for rate, the equation will need to be rearranged to $r = d/t$.

Interest problems

Some word problems will require you to calculate the amount of interest that accrues on a given amount of money over a certain amount of time. In order to solve these problems, you will need to know the equation $I = prt$, in which I is interest, p is principle, r is rate of interest and t is time. Imagine the following scenario: $20 is placed into an account with an annual interest rate of 5%. How much interest will the money have accrued over 5 years? The principal is $20, the interest rate is 5% (for the purposes of calculation you will want to convert the percentage into a decimal, so 5% becomes 0.05), and the time is 5, so the equation can be set up: $I = 20 \times 0.05 \times 5$, yielding an answer of $5. Remember to make sure that if the interest rate is annual, the time needs to be in units of years as well (for instance, six months would become 0.5). Do not worry about compound interest or variable rates; the interest-related questions on the exam do not get so complex.

Graphs

The graphs used on the exam will be of the kinds most familiar to students: circle/pie graph, double axis line graph, triple axis line graph, and bar graph. Remember that on a circle or pie graph, the circle itself represents 1, or 100%. A double axis graph, otherwise known as a line graph, has a horizontal and a vertical axis, each of which represent an individual variable. A triple axis graph has an additional vertical axis on the right side, which is used to mark a third variable. A bar graph is composed of vertical or horizontal bars representing certain values. In rare cases, a question may include two kinds of graphs. When confronting this sort of problem, be sure that the units and scale used by the two graphs are consistent. If they are not, you will need to make adjustments in order to make accurate comparisons of data from each of the graphs.

Measurement conversions

It is very likely that you will confront a few questions asking you to convert one kind of unit(s) into another. At the beginning of the exam, you will be given a list of several equivalencies: 12 inches = 1 foot, 3 feet = 1 yard, 1 centimeter = 0.394 inches, etc. You may then be asked to convert a given amount in one unit to the same amount in another unit. Some of these will be very easy, as for instance: *Convert 3 feet into inches.* To solve this and other problems of this type, simply set up a ratio equation: 1 foot/12 inches = 3 feet/x inches. This equation says, 1 foot is to twelve inches as 3 feet is to x number of inches. To solve, simply cross multiply to derive: $x = 36$. In other words, 3 feet is equal to 36 inches.

On occasion, you will be given a problem that requires you to make more than one step. For instance, using the equivalencies listed above, consider the following question: how many centimeters are in two feet? We do not have a direct equivalency between feet and centimeters, so we will have to make two steps: convert feet into inches and inches into centimeters. The first equation is easy: 1 foot/12 inches = 2 feet/ x inches. Cross-multiplying, we end up with 2 feet = 24 inches. Now, we can set up a similar equation to convert inches into centimeters: 0.394 inches/1 centimeter = 24 inches/x centimeters. Because of the decimal, this calculation will be a bit more messy, but cross-multiplying should yield: $0.394x = 24$. Now, both sides of the equation must be divided by 0.394, yielding roughly 61. In other words, 2 feet = 24 inches = 61 centimeters. When confronted with a problem like this that requires you to take more than one step, remember to go slow and break the problem down into its component parts.

Background and Opinion Questionnaire

Along with the four test sections of the MASS exam, you will be given a background and opinion questionnaire. This questionnaire has been developed specifically for the MASS exam. The main point of the questionnaire is to get an idea of your personality and character traits. It contains questions about your previous job experiences, personal history, and opinions. You will be asked to give short and direct responses to each question. Although there is no specific time limit for completion of the questionnaire, it should take you around 30 minutes.

Because the background and opinion questionnaire is not an aptitude test, the test administrator declares that it is not necessary to prepare for it. In a general sense, this is true: you should know the answer to every question on the questionnaire without preparation. However, there are a few things you should know before you take the questionnaire so that you can make the best possible impression. The avowed intention of the questionnaire is to measure the following characteristics: persistence; conscientiousness; sociability; and the ability to work under adverse conditions. As much as possible, then, you should strive to indicate that you have these characteristics as you give your answers.

For instance, you will almost certainly be required to answer some questions regarding your past job history. When doing so, try to accentuate the positive aspects. If you held a position of leadership, or a position that required you to work closely with others, be sure to mention it. If your job required you to endure adverse conditions or demonstrate a great deal of persistence, do not omit this information. In order to serve as a maintenance worker, you'll have to work in cooperation with a number of other employees; it is a good idea to mention how you have successfully cooperated with others in the past.

Of course, you should not lie or fail to mention any problems in your personal or job history. Most employers will perform a comprehensive background check, and therefore any falsehoods entered in the background and opinion questionnaire will be discovered during the application process. If you have held a number of different jobs, or been fired from a job, simply admit it and describe how you have learned from the experience. Long explanations or excuses will not impress the exam administrator; instead, he or she will want to hear the lessons you have taken from adverse experiences. If you can demonstrate a willingness to grow as a person after negative events (even those of your own doing), you will make a good impression.

While some of the questions on the background and opinion questionnaire will deal directly with your past experiences, others will attempt to probe your opinions on subjects related to life and work. As you answer these questions, remember that your goal is to secure employment, not to impress the exam administrator with your wit and sense of humor. Whenever possible, try to answer questions in terms of how they will affect your ability to do the job. Some questions may describe hypothetical scenarios, and ask you to indicate the best course of action to take in response. These questions will not require any technical knowledge, but rather will ask you to detail your response to a given problem. When doing so, try to remember your responsibilities as an employee as well as your responsibilities to other people.

As an example, imagine that an item on the questionnaire describes a situation in which one of your coworkers repeatedly makes suggestive remarks to another employee in your presence. The questionnaire will then ask you what your response to this situation would be. Obviously, this is a touchy situation. Many people would consider their own interests above those of the organization and more of their fellow employees, and would simply mind their own business. However, it is well-known that sexual-harassment not only decreases productivity but demeans everyone involved. In other words, it is your responsibility to go to your employer and to your coworkers to immediately alert a supervisor to any problematic behavior. By remaining mute on the subject, you are damaging the company and alienating your fellow employees.

Any number of scenarios of this kind may appear on your background and opinion questionnaire. As you answer them, avoid using any language that could be construed as racist, sexist or hateful. Furthermore, to avoid confusion, you should never make jokes during the questionnaire. Try to make your answers clear and direct; one negative tendency the exam administrators will be looking for is equivocation, or the tendency to argue both sides. After you answer each question, read back over your response to make sure it is comprehensible and unequivocal.

In general, the most important quality you can present in the background and opinion questionnaire is optimism. You will not be expected to have a perfect background or to have every opinion in common with your fellow employees. You will, however, be expected to work with a positive attitude and to show respect to your employers and coworkers. Whenever possible, try to make your positivity shine through in your responses. If you indicate a sincere willingness to work hard and learn from your mistakes, you will no doubt make a good impression on the exam administrator.

Practice Test

Practice Questions

Mathematical Usage

Use the information below to answer questions 1-18:

1 acre = 43,560 square feet
1 barrel = 42 gallons
1 fathom = 6 feet
1 foot = 12 inches
1 furlong = 40 rods
1 gallon = 3.785 liters
1 gallon = 4 quarts
1 hand = 10 centimeters
1 inch = 2.54 centimeters
1 kilogram = 1,000 grams
1 kilogram = 2.2 pounds
1 kilometer = 1,000 meters
1 mile = 1.609 kilometers
1 mile = 5,280 feet
3 mile/hour = 4.4 feet/second
1 pint = 4 gills
1 pound = 16 ounces
1 quart = 2 pints
1 slug = 14.59 kilograms
1 square mile = 640 acres

1. 6 kilograms = ? pounds
   a. 2.205
   b. 6,000
   c. 15.24
   d. 13.23

2. 4 furlongs = ? rods
   a. 160
   b. 10
   c. 40
   d. 0.1

3. 80 ounces = ? pounds
   a. 5
   b. 16
   c. 8
   d. 10

4. 3 acres = ? square feet
  a. 43,560
  b. 1,920
  c. 130,680
  d. 640

5. 2 miles = ? kilometers
  a. 1.609
  b. 3.218
  c. 1.243
  d. 2.486

6. 3 quart = ? gallons
  a. 0.33
  b. 4
  c. 1.33
  d. 0.75

7. 12 fathoms = ? feet
  a. 2
  b. 12
  c. 72
  d. 6

8. 126 gallons = ? barrels
  a. 3
  b. 4
  c. 42
  d. 5292

9. 60 miles/hour = ? feet/second
  a. 5
  b. 100
  c. 41
  d. 88

10. 500 grams = ? kilograms
  a. 500,000
  b. 0.5
  c. 50
  d. 0.05

11. 15 hands = ? centimeters
  a. 38
  b. 1.5
  c. 60
  d. 150

12. 15.14 liters = ? gallons
   a. 2
   b. 3
   c. 4
   d. 5

13. 2 barrels = ? quarts
   a. 336
   b. 21
   c. 168
   d. 672

14. 1 mile = ? centimeters
   a. 849,733,632
   b. 160,934
   c. 13,411
   d. 30.5

15. 13.2 pounds = ? grams
   a. 6
   b. 60
   c. 600
   d. 6,000

16. 8 fathoms = ? inches
   a. 96
   b. 48
   c. 576
   d. 4,608

17. 8 quarts = ? liters
   a. 7.57
   b. 121.12
   c. 15.14
   d. 0.53

18. 5 feet = ? centimeters
   a. 12.7
   b. 23.6
   c. 152.4
   d. 60

Reading for Comprehension

Questions 1-10 pertain to the following passage:

Comets

Comets are bodies that orbit the sun. They are distinguishable from asteroids by the presence of coma or tails. In the outer solar system, comets remain frozen and are so small that they are difficult to detect from Earth. As a comet approaches the inner solar system, solar radiation causes the materials within the comet to vaporize and trail off the nuclei. The released dust and gas forms a fuzzy atmosphere called the coma, and the force exerted on the coma causes a tail to form, pointing away from the sun.

Comet nuclei are made of ice, dust, rock and frozen gases and vary widely in size: from 100 meters or so to tens of kilometers across. The comas may be even larger than the Sun. Because of their low mass, they do not become spherical and have irregular shapes.

There are over 3,500 known comets, and the number is steadily increasing. This represents only a small portion of the total comets existing, however. Most comets are too faint to be visible without the aid of a telescope; the number of comets visible to the naked eye is around one a year.
Comets leave a trail of solid debris behind them. If a comet's path crosses the Earth's path, there will likely be meteor showers as Earth passes through the trail of debris.

Many comets and asteroids have collided into Earth. Some scientists believe that comets hitting Earth about 4 billion years ago brought a significant proportion of the water in Earth's oceans. There are still many near-Earth comets.

Most comets have oval shaped orbits that take them close to the Sun for part of their orbit and then out further into the Solar System for the remainder of the orbit. Comets are often classified according to the length of their orbital period: short period comets have orbital periods of less than 200 years, long period comets have orbital periods of more than 200 years, single apparition comets have trajectories which cause them to permanently leave the solar system after passing the Sun once.

1. What does the passage not list as a component of comet nuclei?
   a. solar radiation
   b. dust
   c. frozen gases
   d. rock

2. According to the passage, what do some scientists believe brought a significant proportion of the water in the Earth's oceans?
   a. Comets' released gas and dust
   b. Comets exiting in the solar system
   c. Comet collisions with the Sun
   d. Comet collisions with Earth

3. What does the passage claim distinguishes comets from asteroids?
   a. The make-up of their nuclei
   b. The presence of coma or tails
   c. Their orbital periods
   d. Their irregular shapes

4. What would a comet with an orbital period of 1,000 years be called?
   a. a short period comet
   b. a long period comet
   c. a single apparition comet
   d. an elliptical comet

5. According to the passage, which of the following is true?
   a. There are 350 known comets and the number is steadily increasing.
   b. There are 3,500 known comets and the number is staying the same.
   c. There are 3,500 known comets and many more comets that aren't known.
   d. Most comets are visible to the naked eye.

6. According to the passage, what makes up the coma?
   a. released dust and gas
   b. a meteor shower
   c. asteroids
   d. rock

7. According to the passage, why do comets have irregular shapes?
   a. because they are not spherical
   b. because they have orbital periods
   c. because of their low mass
   d. because of their tails

8. What does the passage claim about the size of comets?
   a. Some are tens of kilometers across and the coma can be larger than the Sun
   b. Some are tens of kilometers across and the coma is never larger than the Sun
   c. Some are 100 meters across and the coma is never larger than the Sun
   d. The smallest comet is at least a kilometer and the coma can be larger than the Sun

9. According to the passage, what shape is the orbit of most comets?
   a. circular
   b. square
   c. linear
   d. oval

10. According to the passage, why are comets in the outer solar system difficult to detect from Earth?

a. They are not in orbit.
b. They are frozen.
c. They have irregular shapes.
d. They are small.

Questions 11-17 pertain to the following passage:

Cilia and Flagella

Cilia and flagella are tubular structures found on the surfaces of many animal cells. They are examples of organelles, sub-cellular structures that perform a particular function. By beating against the surrounding medium in a swimming motion, they may endow cells with motility or induce the medium to circulate, as in the case of gills. Ciliated cells typically each contain large numbers of cilia 2 -10 μm (micrometer) long. In contrast, flagellated cells usually have one or two flagella, and the structures can be as long as 200 μm. For both types of structure, the diameters are less than 0.5 μm.

Although they share similar structures, the motion of the two organelles is somewhat different. Flagella beat in a circular, undulating motion that is continuous. The effective stroke of a cilium's beat, which generates the power, is followed by a more languid recovery to the original position. During the recovery stroke, they are brought in close to the membrane of the cell. Cilia usually beat in coordinated waves, so that at any given moment some are in the midst of their power stroke while others are recovering. This provides for a steady flow of fluid past gill surfaces or the epithelia lining the lungs or digestive tract.

The construction of both organelles is very similar. A portion of the cell membrane appears to be stretched over a framework made of tubulin polymers. A polymer is a long, chain-like molecule made of smaller units that are strung together. In this case, the subunits are molecules of the protein tubulin. The framework, or skeleton, of a cilium or flagellum consists of 9 pairs of tubulin polymers spaced around the periphery, and two more single polymers of tubulin that run along the center of the shaft. This is called a 9+2 pattern.

The motion of the organelles results from chemical reactions that cause the outer polymers to slide past one another. By doing so, they force the overall structure to bend. This is similar to the mechanism of contraction of skeletal muscle. In cilia and flagella, the nine outer polymer pairs of the skeleton have along their lengths molecules of a rod-shaped protein called dynein. The dynein rods can grasp, or bind to, the neighboring tubulin polymer. Energy is then used to drive a chemical reaction that causes the dynein arms to bend, causing one tubulin polymer to move along the length of the other. Through a coordinated series of thousands of such reactions, the cilium or flagellum will beat.

11. Cilia and flagella are both
   a. Proteins.
   b. Sub-cellular structures that perform a particular function.
   c. Organelles that beat in a continuous undulating motion.
   d. Single-celled protists

12. According to the passage, where would you expect to find cilia?
   a. Stomach lining
   b. Back of the hand
   c. Lining of the heart
   d. Circulatory system

13. According to the passage, how many tubulin polymers make up the entire 9+2 pattern seen in cilia and flagella?
   a. 11
   b. 9
   c. 20
   d. Passage doesn't say

14. Two proteins mentioned in this passage are
   a. Tubulin and Paramecium.
   b. Tubulin and dynein.
   c. Tubulin and flagellin.
   d. Tubulin and Sonneborn.

15. Which of the following describes how the beating motion of flagella is caused?
   a. The two central polymers slide past one another.
   b. Dynein causes the outer polymer pairs to slide past one another.
   c. Dynein causes each of the outer polymers to bend.
   d. The organelle increases in diameter.

16. Polymers are always
   a. Made of protein.
   b. Made of tubulin.
   c. Made of subunits.
   d. Arranged in a 9+2 array.

17. The passage describes cilia and flagella and tells us that
   a. Cilia may be 200 μm long.
   b. Flagella are less than 0.5 μm long.
   c. Cells can have more than two flagella.
   d. Flagella are less than 0.5 μm in diameter.

Questions 18-25 pertain to the following passage:

Daylight Savings Time

Daylight Saving Time (DST) is the practice of changing clocks so that afternoons have more daylight and mornings have less. Clocks are adjusted forward one hour in the spring and one hour backward in the fall. The main purpose of the change is to make better use of daylight.

DST began with the goal of conservation. Benjamin Franklin suggested it as a method of saving on candles. It was used during both World Wars to save energy for military needs. Although DST's potential to save energy was a primary reason behind its implementation, research into its effects on energy conservation are contradictory and unclear.

Beneficiaries of DST include all activities that can benefit from more sunlight after working hours, such as shopping and sports. A 1984 issue of Fortune magazine estimated that a seven-week extension of DST would yield an additional $30 million for 7-Eleven stores. Public safety may be increased by the use of DST: some research suggests that traffic fatalities may be reduced when there is additional afternoon sunlight.

On the other hand, DST complicates timekeeping and some computer systems. Tools with built-in time-keeping functions such as medical devices can be affected negatively. Agricultural and evening entertainment interests have historically opposed DST.

DST can affect health, both positively and negatively. It provides more afternoon sunlight in which to get exercise. It also impacts sunlight exposure; this is good for getting vitamin D, but bad in that it can increase skin cancer risk. DST may also disrupt sleep.

Today, daylight saving time has been adopted by more than one billion people in about 70 countries. DST is generally not observed in countries near the equator because sunrise times do not vary much there. Asia and Africa do not generally observe it. Some countries, such as Brazil, observe it only in some regions.

DST can lead to peculiar situations. One of these occurred in November, 2007 when a woman in North Carolina gave birth to one twin at 1:32 a.m. and, 34 minutes later, to the second twin. Because of DST and the time change at 2:00 a.m., the second twin was officially born at 1:06, 26 minutes earlier than her brother.

18. According to the passage, what is the main purpose of DST?
    a. To increase public safety
    b. To benefit retail businesses
    c. To make better use of daylight
    d. To promote good health

19. Which of the following is not mentioned in the passage as a negative effect of DST?
   a. Energy conservation
   b. Complications with time keeping
   c. Complications with computer systems
   d. Increased skin cancer risk

20. The article states that DST involves:
   a. Adjusting clocks forward one hour in the spring and the fall.
   b. Adjusting clocks backward one hour in the spring and the fall.
   c. Adjusting clocks forward in the fall and backward in the spring.
   d. Adjusting clocks forward in the spring and backward in the fall.

21. Which interests have historically opposed DST, according to the passage?
   a. retail businesses and sports
   b. evening entertainment and agriculture
   c. 7-Eleven and health
   d. medical devices and computing

22. According to the article, increased sunlight exposure:
   a. is only good for health.
   b. is only bad for health.
   c. has no effect on health.
   d. can be both good and bad for health.

23. Where does the article state DST is observed only in some regions?
   a. Asia
   b. Africa
   c. The United States
   d. Brazil

24. What is an example given in the passage of a peculiar situation that DST has caused?
   a. sleep disruption
   b. driving confusion
   c. twin birth order complications
   d. countries with DST only in certain regions

25. For what purpose did Benjamin Franklin first suggest DST?
   a. to save money for military needs
   b. to save candles
   c. to reduce traffic fatalities
   d. to promote reading

Questions 26-32 pertain to the following passage:

Peanut Allergies

Peanut allergy is the most prevalent food allergy in the United States, affecting around one and a half million people, and it is potentially on the rise in children in the United States. While thought to be the most common cause of food-related death, deaths from food allergies are very rare. The allergy typically begins at a very young age and remains present for life for most people. Approximately one-fifth to one-quarter of children with a peanut allergy, however, outgrow it. Treatment involves careful avoidance of peanuts or any food that may contain peanut pieces or oils. For some sufferers, exposure to even the smallest amount of peanut product can trigger a serious reaction.

Symptoms of peanut allergy can include skin reactions, itching around the mouth, digestive problems, shortness of breath, and runny or stuffy nose. The most severe peanut allergies can result in anaphylaxis, which requires immediate treatment with epinephrine. Up to one-third of people with peanut allergies have severe reactions. Without treatment, anaphylactic shock can result in death due to obstruction of the airway, or heart failure. Signs of anaphylaxis include constriction of airways and difficulty breathing, shock, a rapid pulse, and dizziness or lightheadedness.

As of yet, there is no treatment to prevent or cure allergic reactions to peanuts. In May of 2008, however, Duke University Medical Center food allergy experts announced that they expect to offer a treatment for peanut allergies within five years.

Scientists do not know for sure why peanut proteins induce allergic reactions, nor do they know why some people develop peanut allergies while others do not. There is a strong genetic component to allergies: if one of a child's parents has an allergy, the child has an almost 50% chance of developing an allergy. If both parents have an allergy, the odds increase to about 70%.

Someone suffering from a peanut allergy needs to be cautious about the foods he or she eats and the products he or she puts on his or her skin. Common foods that should be checked for peanut content are ground nuts, cereals, granola, grain breads, energy bars, and salad dressings. Store prepared cookies, pastries, and frozen desserts like ice cream can also contain peanuts. Additionally, many cuisines use peanuts in cooking – watch for peanut content in African, Chinese, Indonesian, Mexican, Thai, and Vietnamese dishes.

Parents of children with peanut allergies should notify key people (child care providers, school personnel, etc.) that their child has a peanut allergy, explain peanut allergy symptoms to them, make sure that the child's epinephrine auto injector is always available, write an action plan of care for their child when he or she has an allergic reaction to peanuts, have their child wear a medical alert bracelet or necklace, and discourage their child from sharing foods.

26. According to the passage, approximately what percentage of people with peanut allergies have severe reactions?
  a. Up to 11%
  b. Up to 22%
  c. Up to 33%
  d. Up to 44%

27. By what year do Duke University allergy experts expect to offer a treatment for peanut allergies?
a. 2008
b. 2010
c. 2012
d. 2013

28. Which of the following is not a type of cuisine the passage suggests often contains peanuts?
a. African
b. Italian
c. Vietnamese
d. Mexican

29. Which allergy does the article state is thought to be the most common cause of food-related death?
a. Peanut
b. Tree nut
c. Bee sting
d. Shellfish

30. It can be inferred from the passage that children with peanut allergies should be discouraged from sharing food because:
a. Peanut allergies can be contagious.
b. People suffering from peanut allergies are more susceptible to bad hygiene.
c. Many foods contain peanut content and it is important to be very careful when you don't know what you're eating.
d. Scientists don't know why some people develop peanut allergies.

31. Which of the following does the passage not state is a sign of anaphylaxis?
a. constriction of airways
b. a rapid pulse
c. dizziness
d. running or stuffy nose

32. According to the passage, what are the approximate odds of a child developing a peanut allergy if only one of the two parents has a peanut allergy?
a. 30%
b. 50%
c. 70%
d. 90%

Assembly

In this portion of the exam test takers need to figure out how an object would look after being properly assembled. The first picture in each problem displays all the parts that need to be assembled. The next five illustrations display five different methods of assembly, four of which are wrong, and one of which is right.

Every part has at least one letter marking it; some have more than one. Each letter represents a place on the assembled part. Some letters are also shown that correspond to unseen areas. These are displayed with a dotted line that points to the side underneath, or the unseen area.

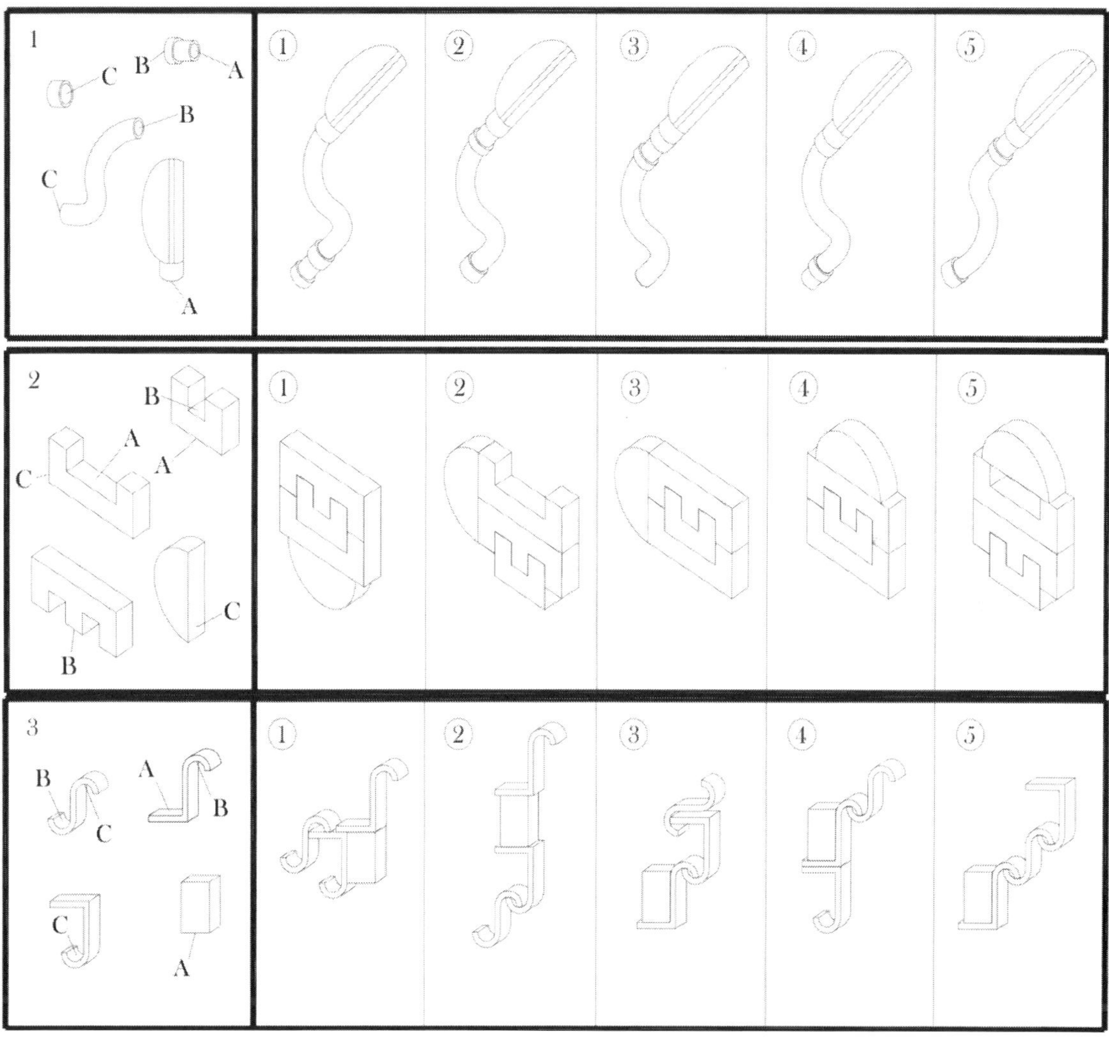

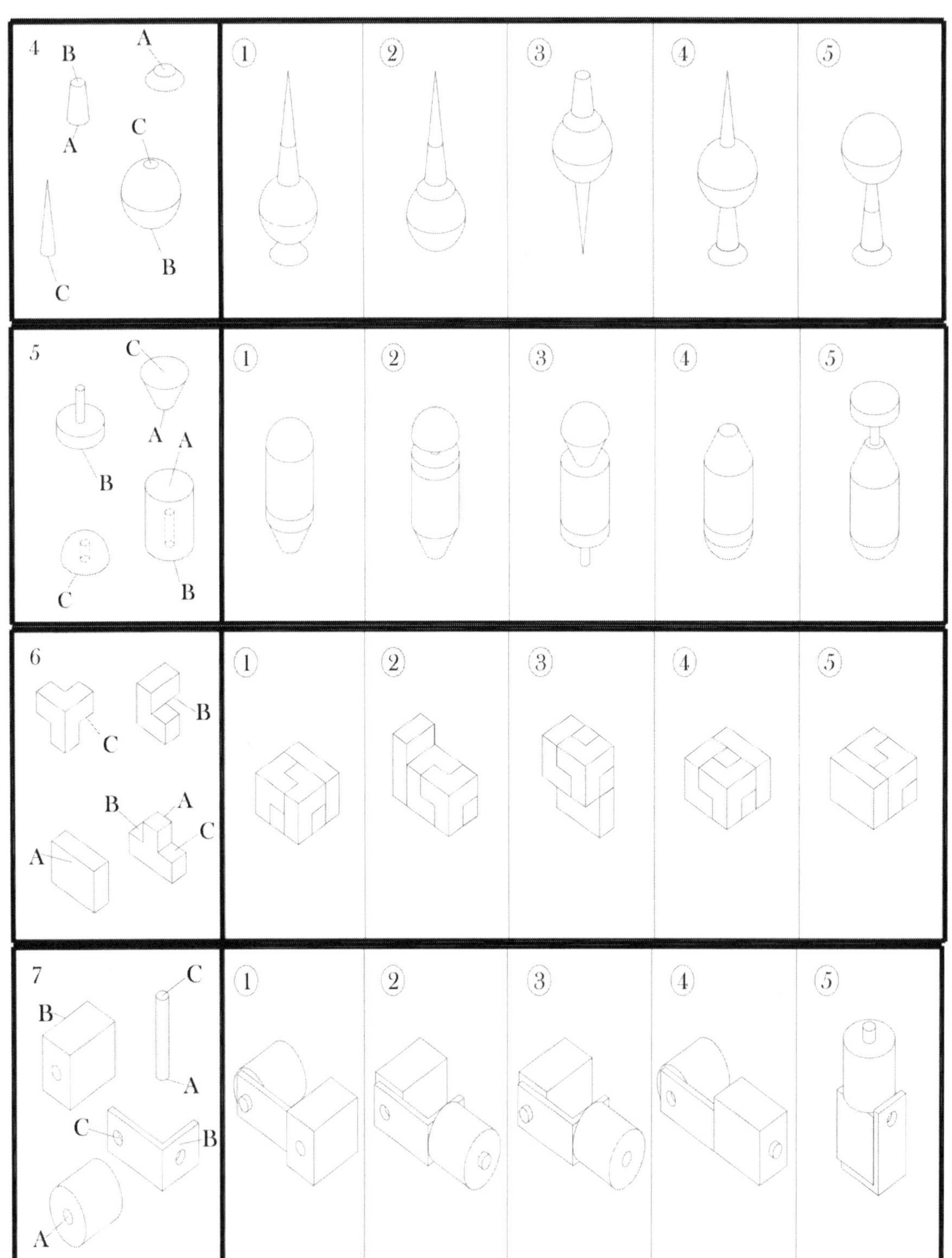
4
B
A
A
C
B
C
1
2
3
4
5
5
C
A
A
B
C
B
1
2
3
4
5
6
B
C
B
A
C
A
1
2
3
4
5
7
C
B
A
C
B
A
1
2
3
4
5

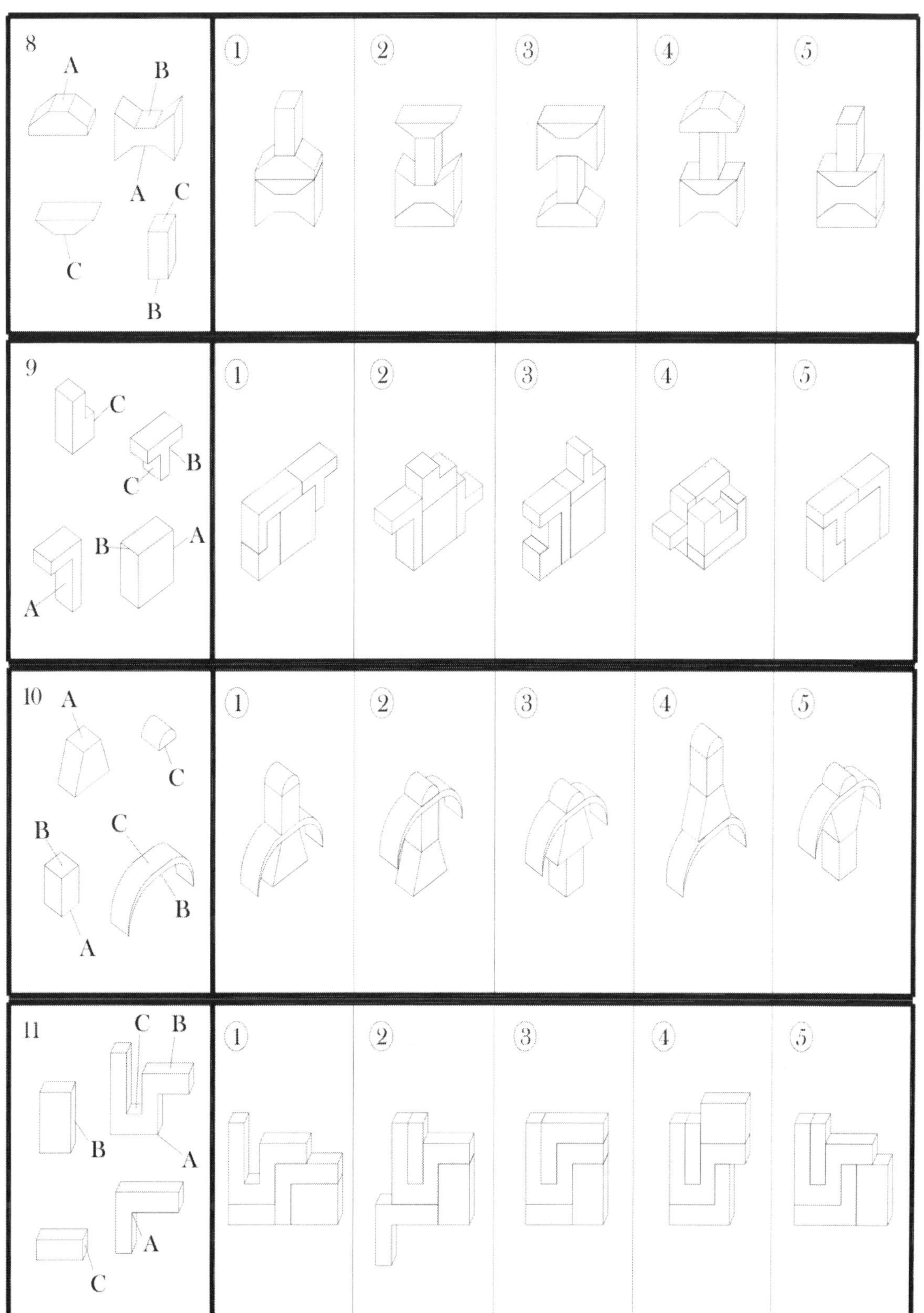

8
A
B
A
C
C
B
1
2
3
4
5
9
C
B
C
B
A
A
1
2
3
4
5
10
A
C
B
C
B
A
1
2
3
4
5
11
C
B
B
A
A
C
1
2
3
4
5

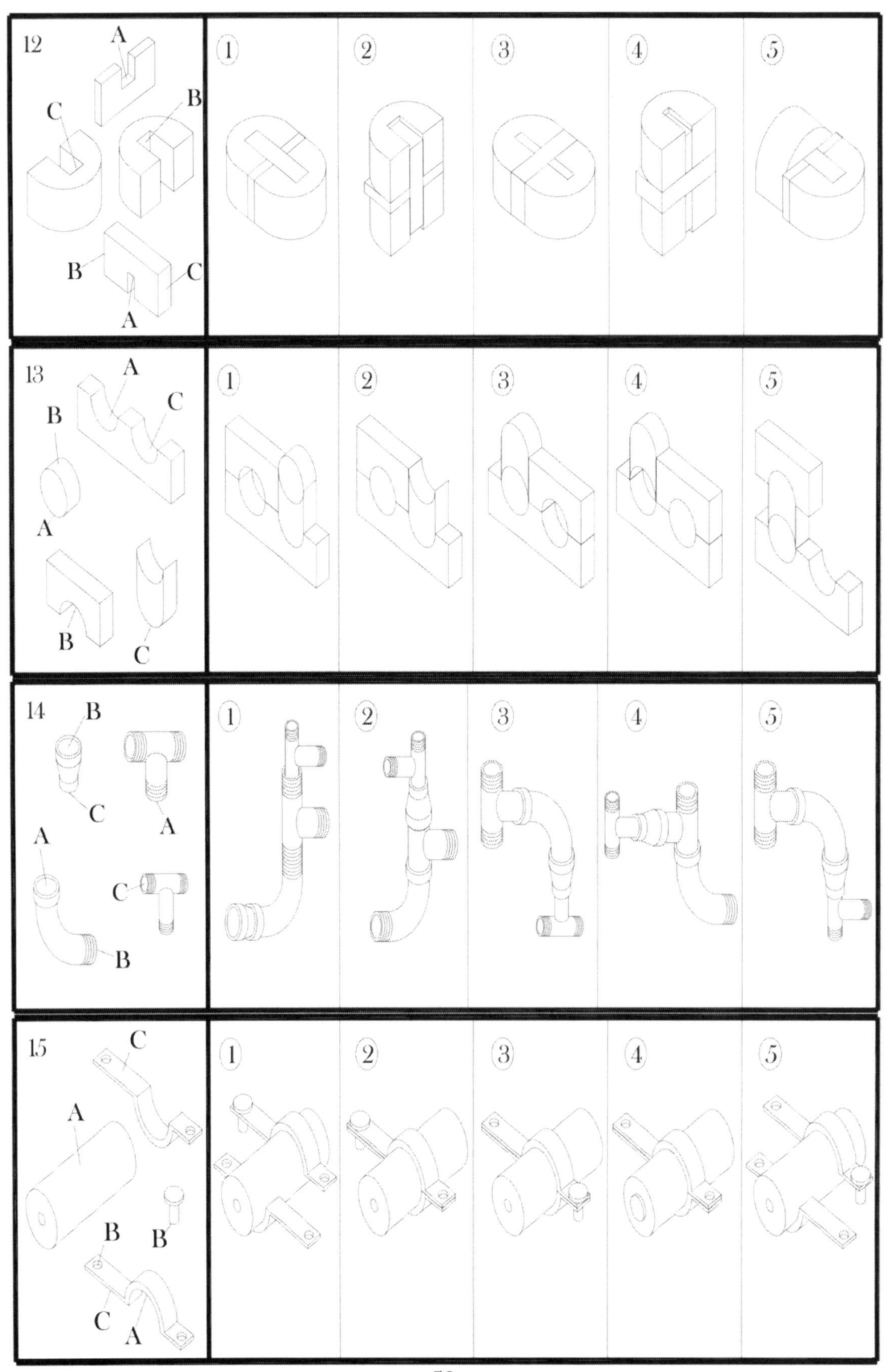
12
A
B
C
B
C
A
1
2
3
4
5
13
A
B
C
A
B
C
1
2
3
4
5
14
B
C
A
A
C
B
1
2
3
4
5
15
C
A
B
B
C
A
1
2
3
4
5

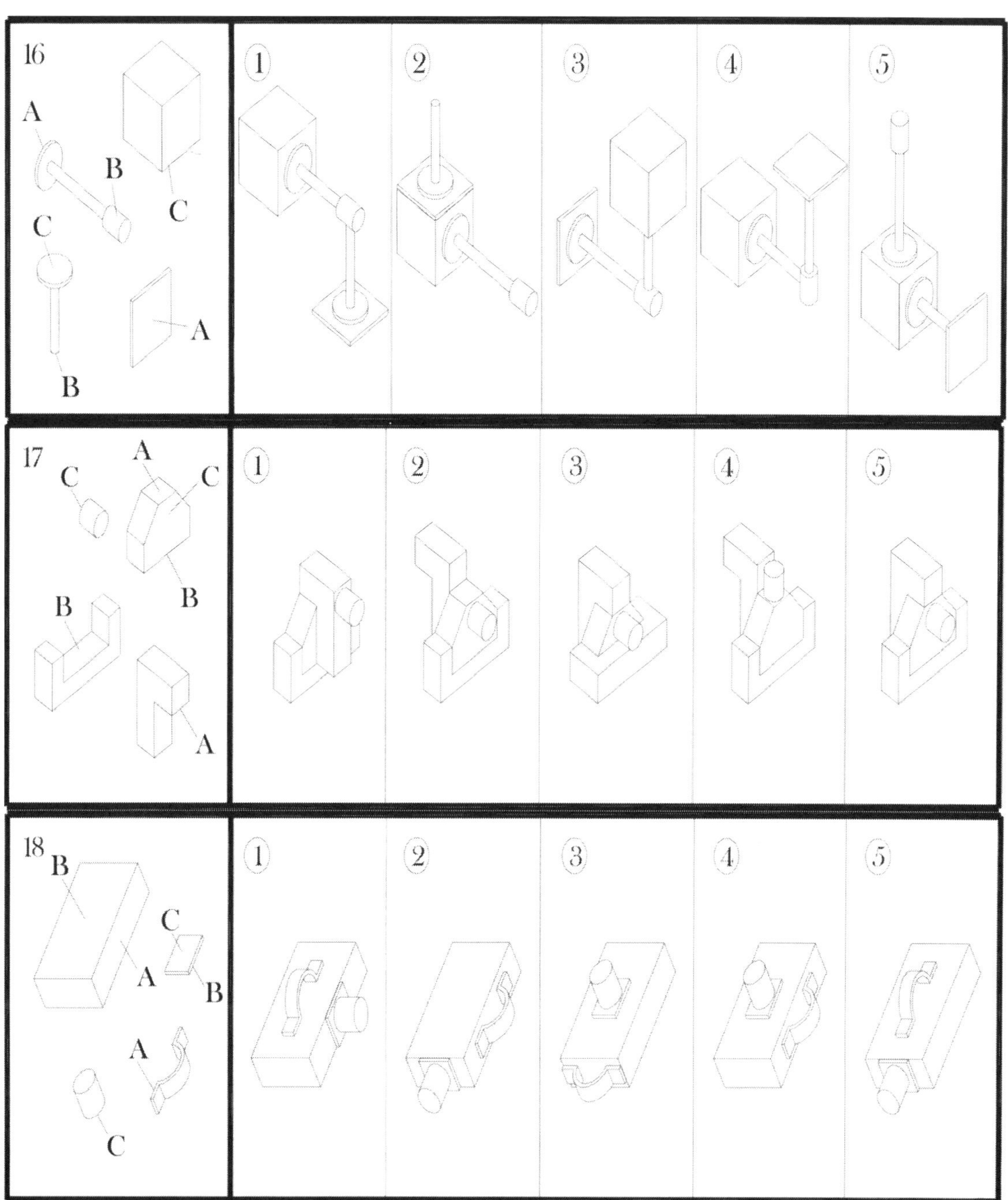
16
A
B
C
C
A
B
1
2
3
4
5
17
A
C
C
B
B
A
1
2
3
4
5
18
B
C
A
B
A
C
1
2
3
4
5

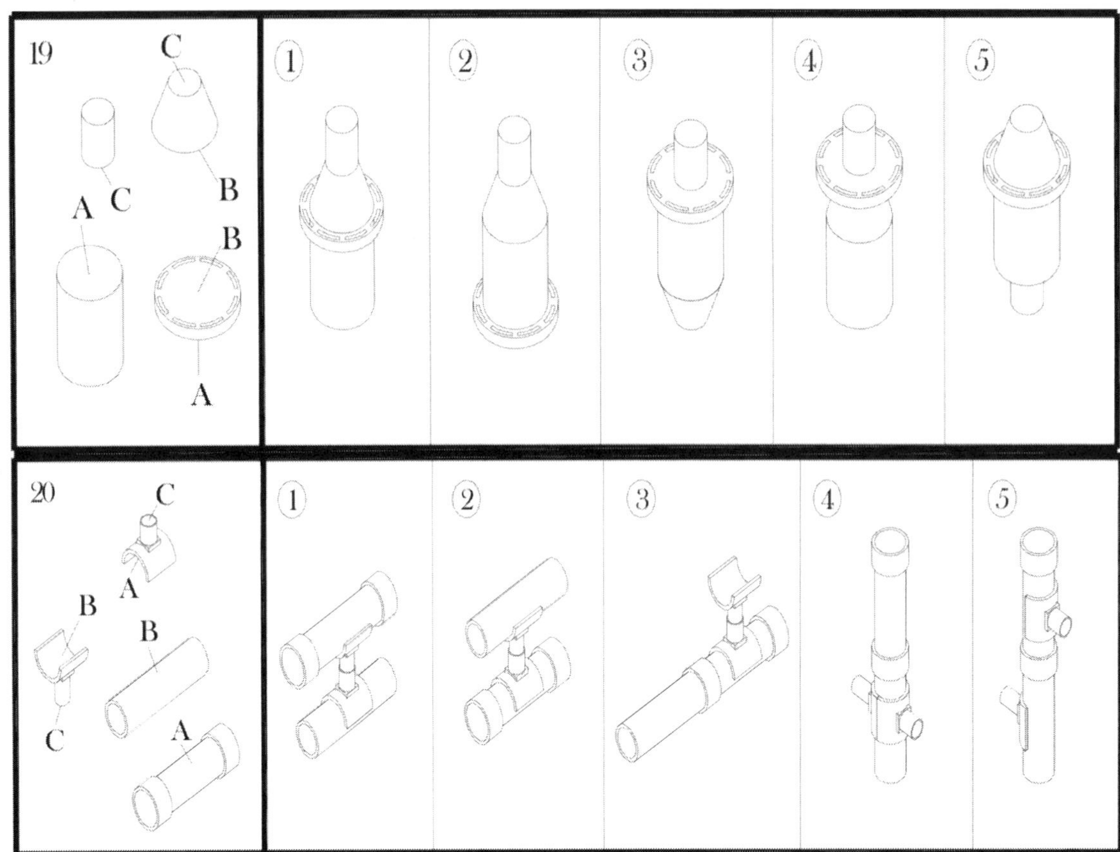
19
C
C
B
A
B
A
1
2
3
4
5
20
C
A
B
B
C
A
1
2
3
4
5

Mechanical Concepts

This is a test of your ability to understand mechanical concepts. Each question has a picture, a question and three possible answers. Read each question carefully, study the picture, and decide which answer is correct.

1. Objects 1 and 2 are submerged in separate tanks, both filled with water. In which tank (A or B) will the water level be the highest? (If equal, mark C)

2. If ball 1 and ball 2 are of equal weight and moving at the same speed, in which direction (A, B or C) will ball 1 tend to go when it collides with ball 2 at point X?

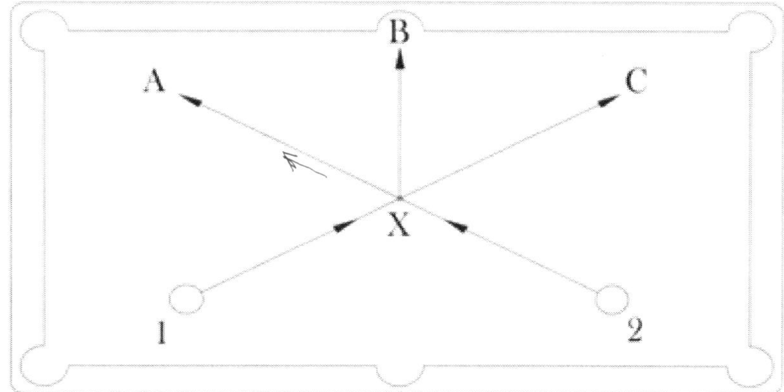

3. In which direction (A or B) will gear 5 spin if gear 1 is spinning counter-clockwise? (If both, mark C)

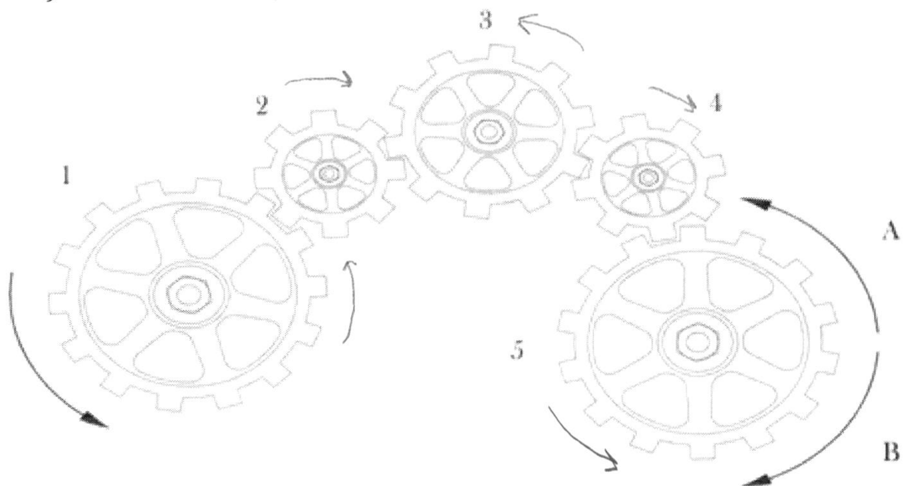

4. Which of the two identical objects (A or B) will launch a higher distance when the springs are released? (If equal, mark C)

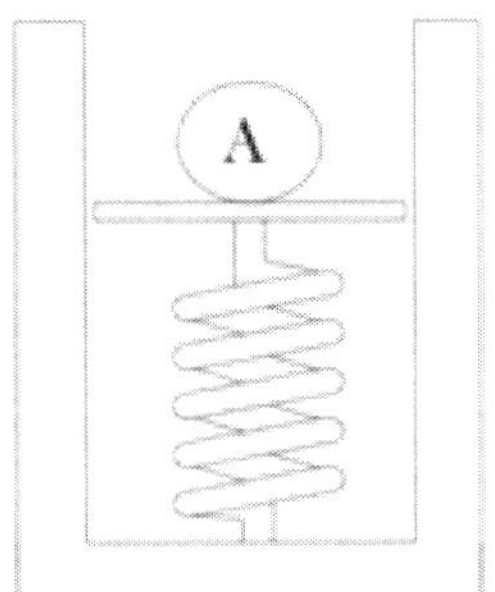

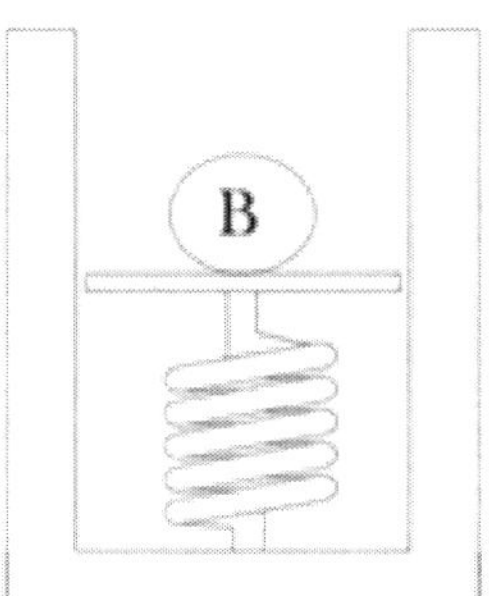

5. A watering can is filled with water. Which of the pictures (A or B) shows a more accurate representation of how the water will rest?

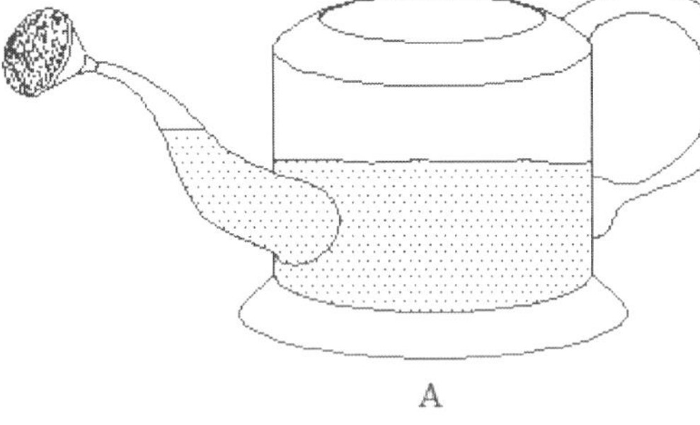
A

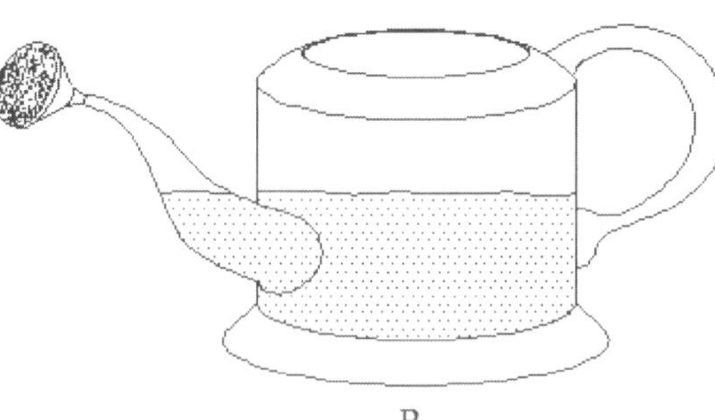
B

6. Among this arrangement of three pulleys, which pulley (A, B or C) turns fastest?

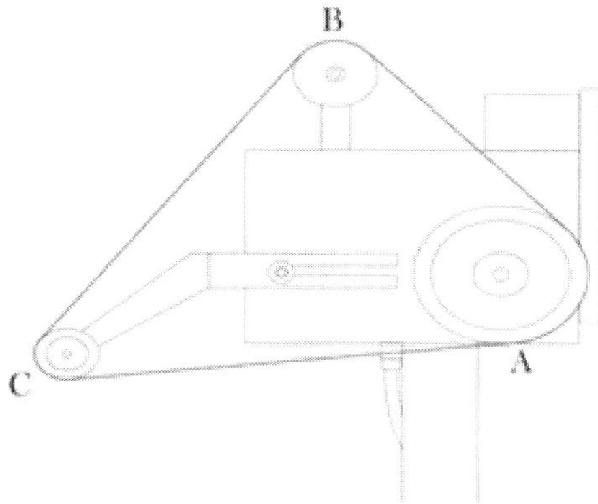

7. Which of the two scenarios (A or B) requires more effort to pull the weight up off the ground? (If equal, mark C)

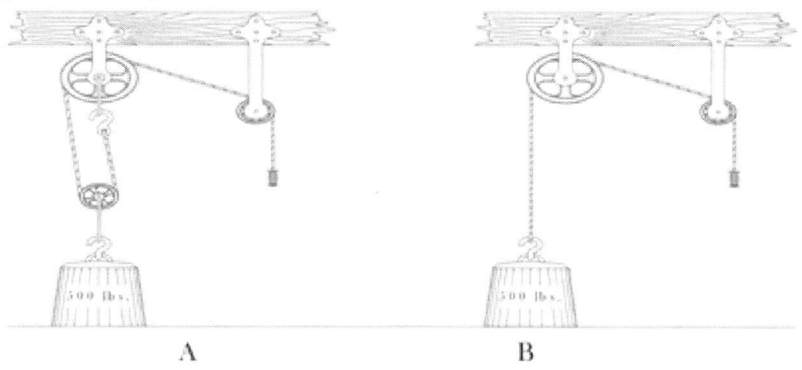

8. Which switch (A, B or C) should be closed in order to start the pump motor?

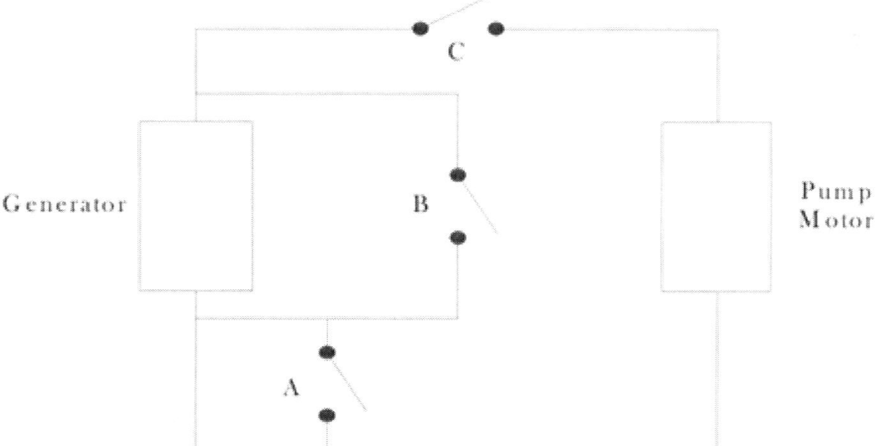

9. Which situation (A or B) requires more force to peddle the bicycle up the ramp? (If equal, mark C)

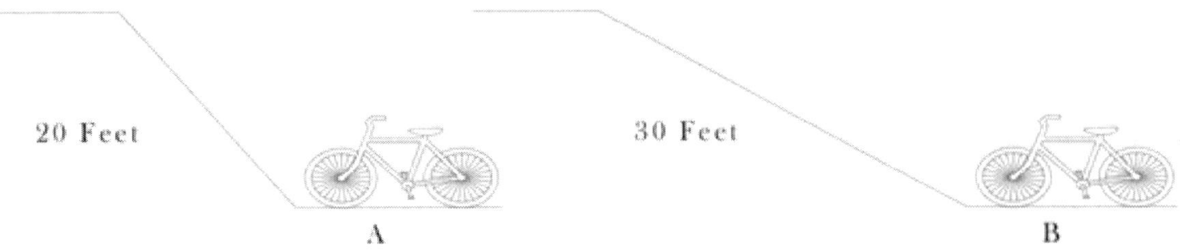

10. When the spring is released, the ball travels away from the spring to its highest point (A) and then begins to travel back towards its place of origin. At which point (A, B or C) will the ball travel to after it hits the spring a second time?

11. Which of the two boulders of equal weight (A or B) requires more force to push up the hill? (If equal, mark C)

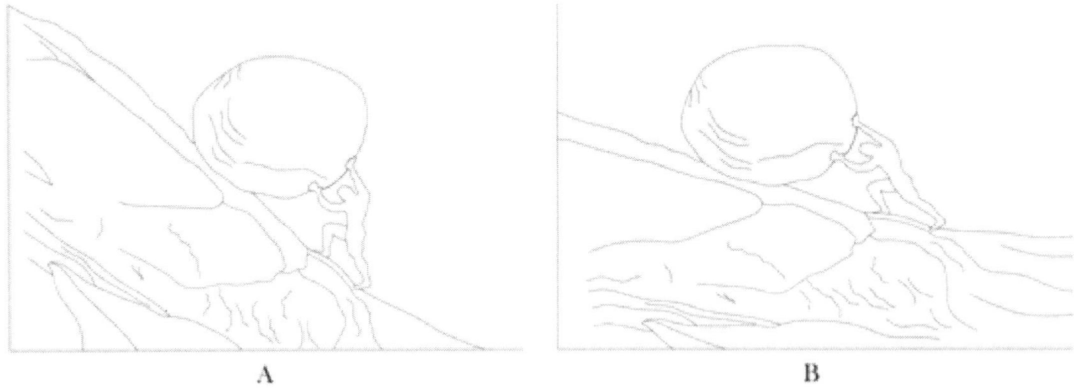

12. At which point (A, B or C) will the cannonball be traveling the slowest?

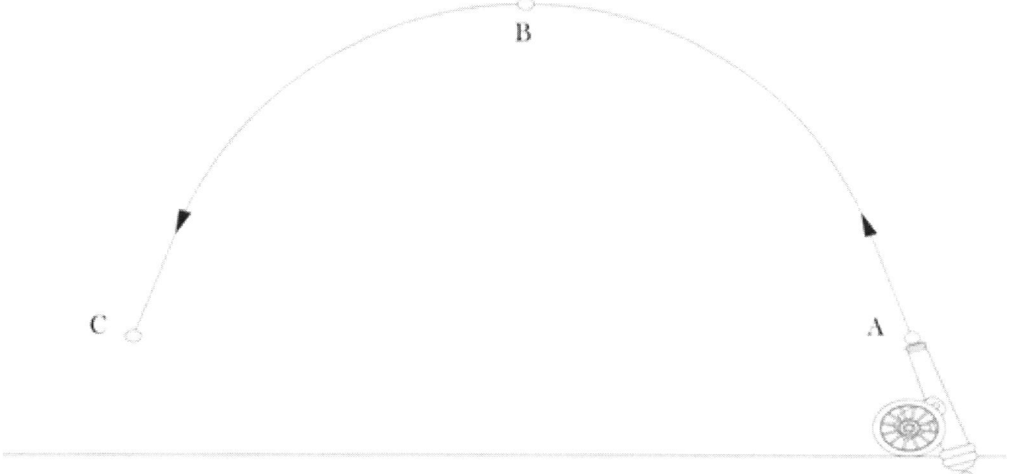

13. On which side of the pipe (A or B) would the water speed be slower? (If equal, mark C)

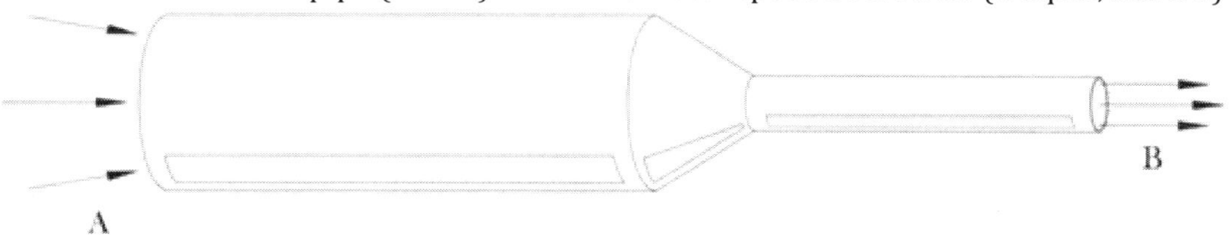

14. In which of the two figures (A or B) is the person bearing more weight? (If equal, mark C)

15. Which of the two lift trucks (A or B) carrying the same amount of weight is more likely to tip over? (If equal, mark C)

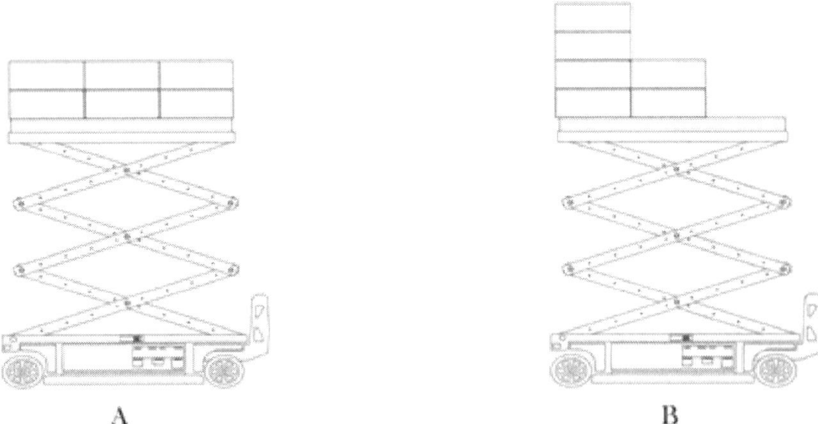

16. The weight of the boxes is being carried by the two men shown below. Which of the two men (A or B) is carrying more weight? (If equal, mark C)

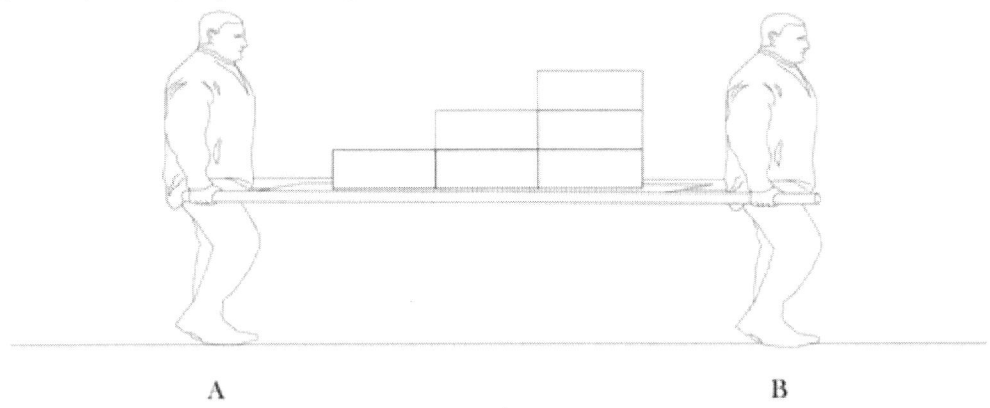

17. In the pictures below, which of the angles (A or B) is braced more solidly? (If equal, mark C)

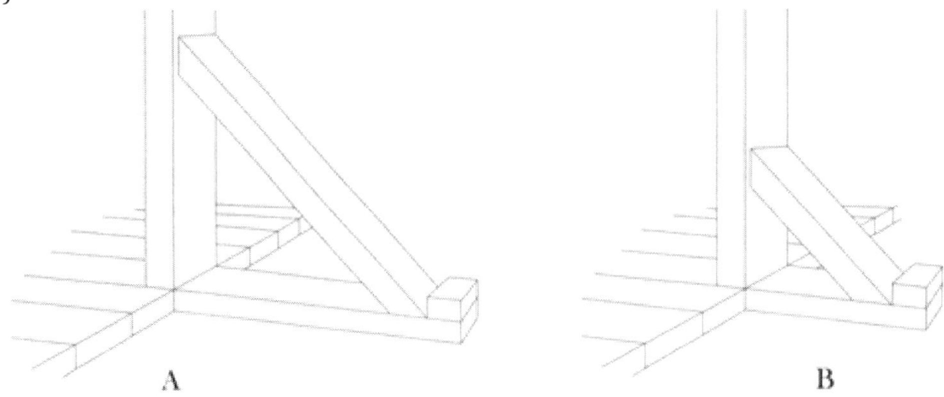

18. Given two birds sitting on branches of a tree at different elevations. Both drop objects of identical size and weight. Which object (A or B) will hit the ground with bigger force? (If equal, mark C)

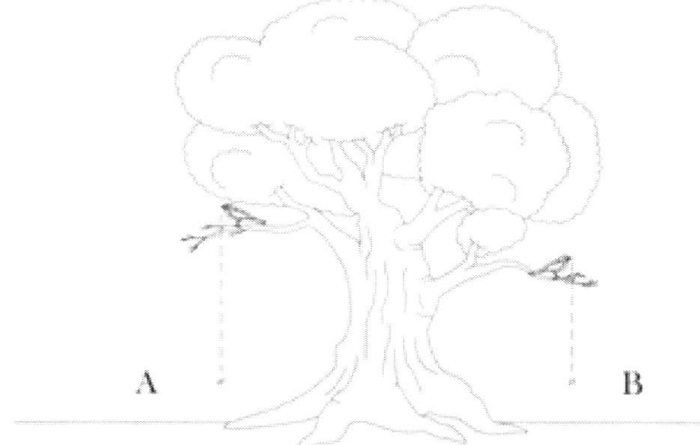

19. Which of the two wagons (A or B) of equal size and weight would be easier to drag up the hill? (If equal, mark C)

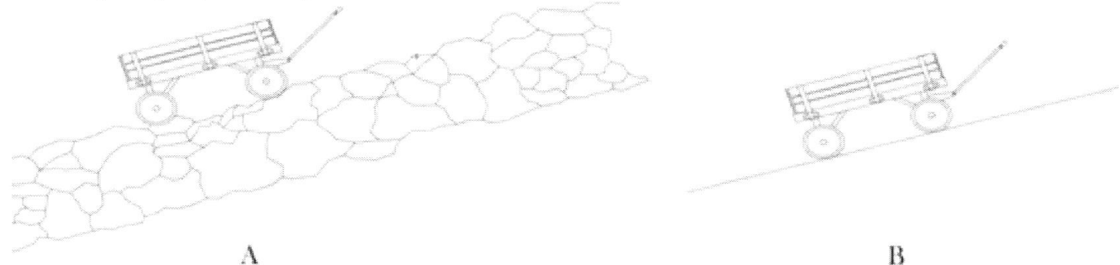

20. In which of the three positions (A, B or C) will it be easiest to accurately measure the amount of liquid in the graduated cylinder?

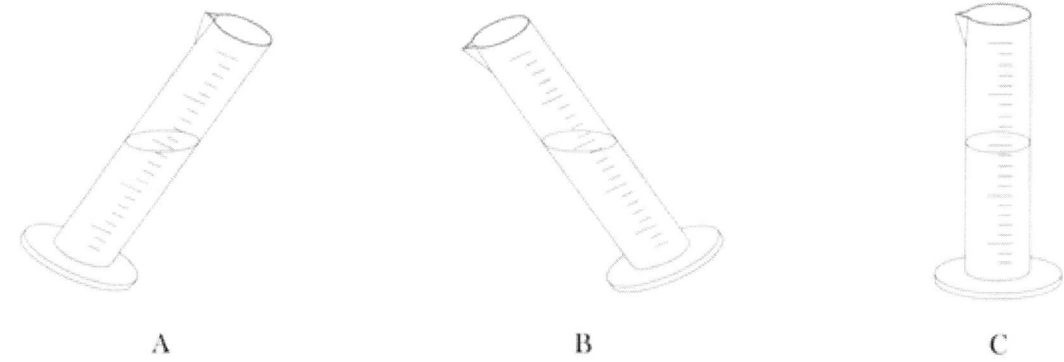

21. In which of the two figures (A or B) will the person require less force to lift a 100 pound weight? (If equal, mark C)

22. Which switch (A, B or C) should be closed to give power to the light?

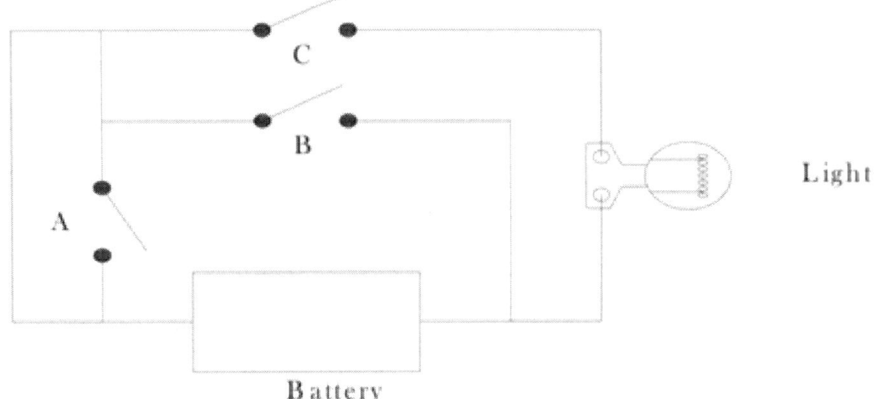

23. If the baseball and bowling ball are moving at the same speed, in which direction will the bowling ball tend to go when it collides with the baseball at point X?

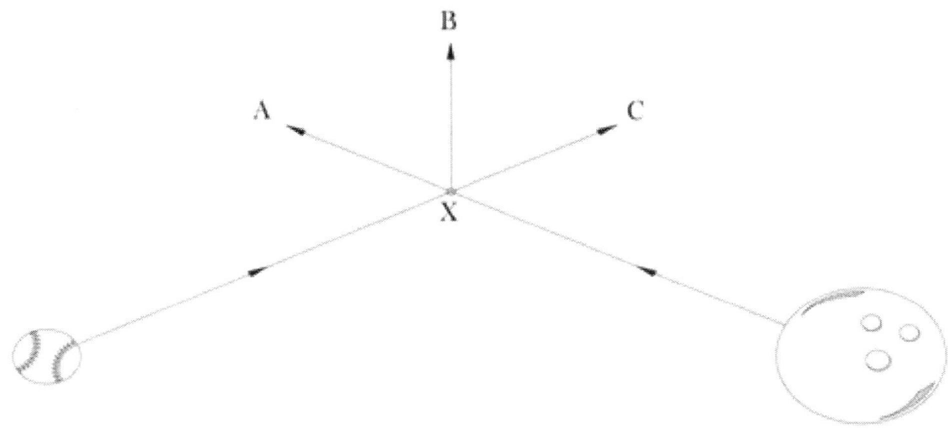

24. Which of the two rolls of paper towels (A or B) will undergo more revolutions if the ends of each roll were pulled downward with the same amount of force? (If equal, mark C)

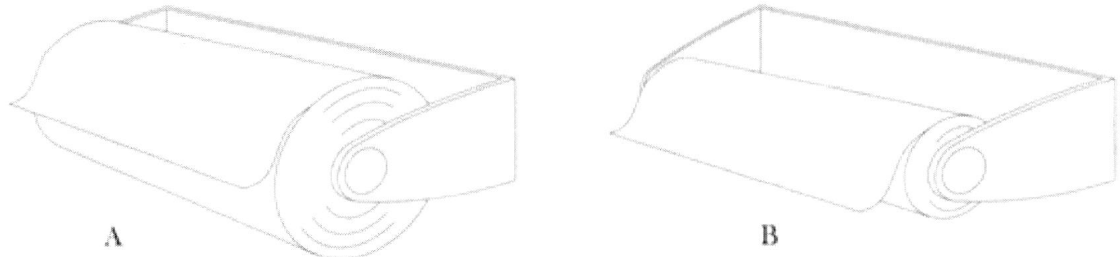

25. In which of the two containers (A or B) will water that is boiled to the same temperature cool more slowly? (If equal, mark C)

26. The water container A contains 50% salt. The water container B contains 25% salt. In which of the two containers (A or B) is an egg more likely to float? (If equal, mark C)

27. Which reflector (A or B) on the bicycle wheel is going to be traveling a greater distance when the wheel turns? (If equal, mark C)

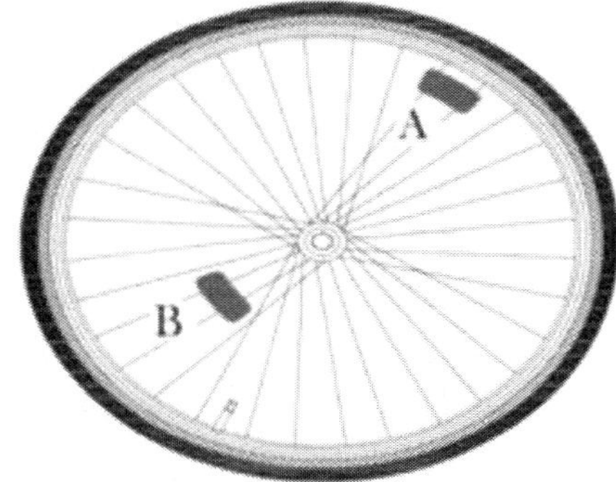

28. A javelin is thrown into the air. At which point (A, B or C) will the javelin be traveling the fastest?

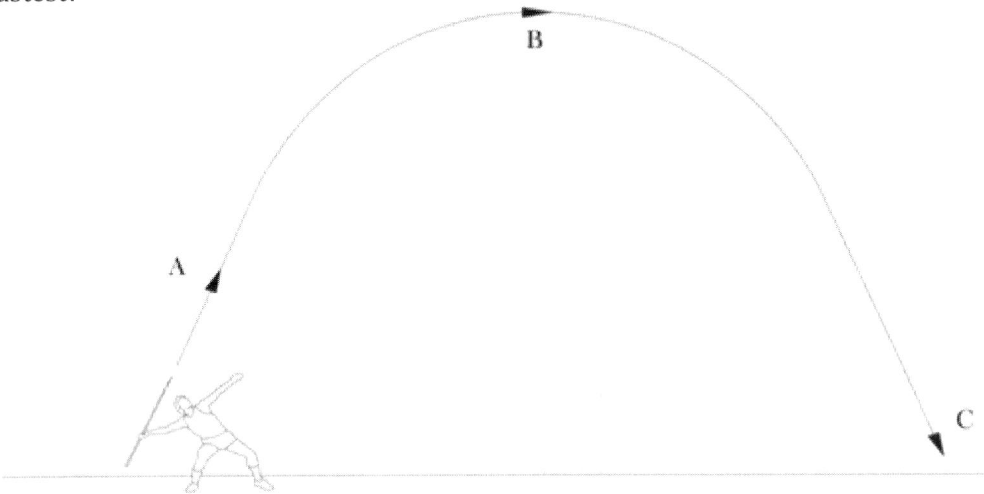

29. A child is released on the seat of a swing set at point (A). At what point (A, B or C) will the child travel to before he/she begins to return back to the point of origin?

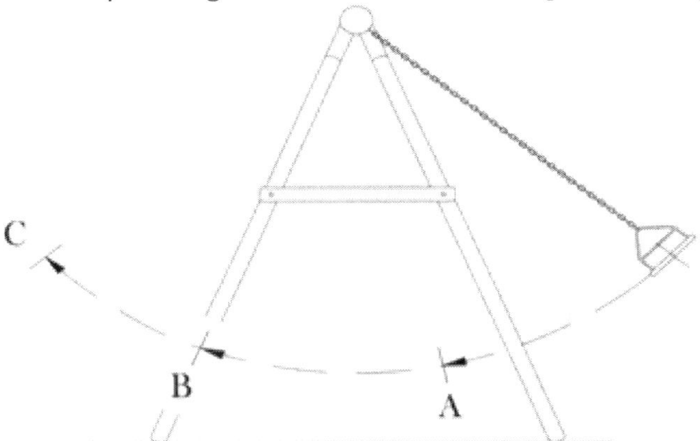

30. On which side of the pipe (A or B) would the water speed be slower? (If equal, mark C)

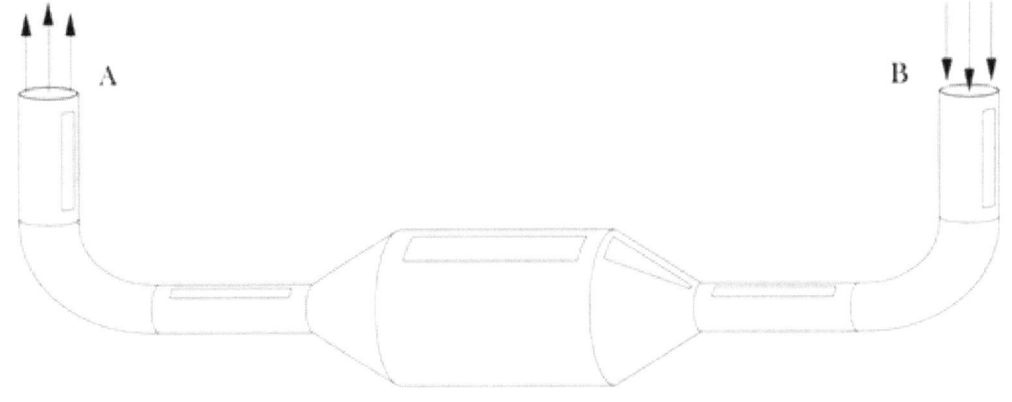

31. Given two objects shown below that are dropped from an elevation of 100 feet. Neglecting air resistance, which object (A or B) will fall at a faster rate? (If equal, mark C)

32. An athlete is holding a heavy metal ball attached to a wire and is rotating in the circular motion shown below. In which direction (A, B or C) would the ball travel when it is released at point X?

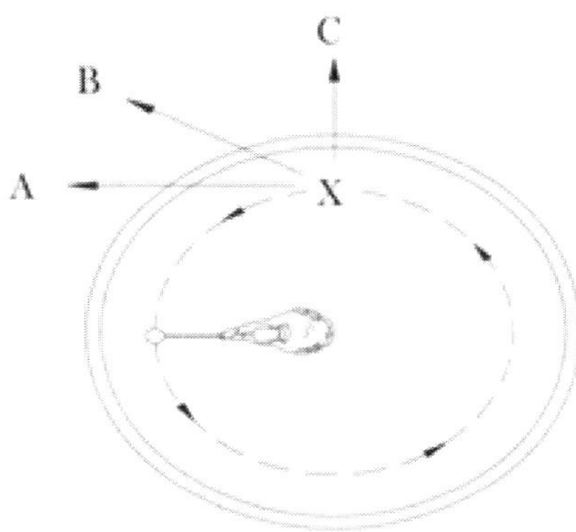

33. Which of the two wheels (A or B) will allow you to travel a further distance given the same rotational speed? (If equal, mark C)

34. Two tanks with different capacities contain the same amount of gas, 50 kg. In which of the given tanks (A or B) will the gas pressure be greater? (If equal, mark C)

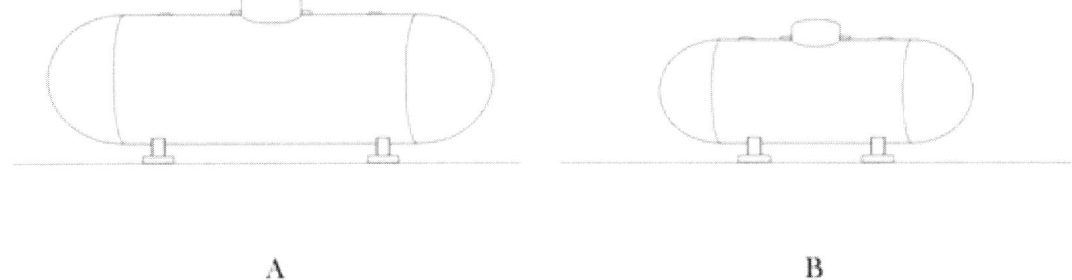

A B

35. Given two water towers with identical tanks and identical amounts of water in each tank, which tower (A or B) will have greater water pressure coming out of the hose? (If equal, mark C)

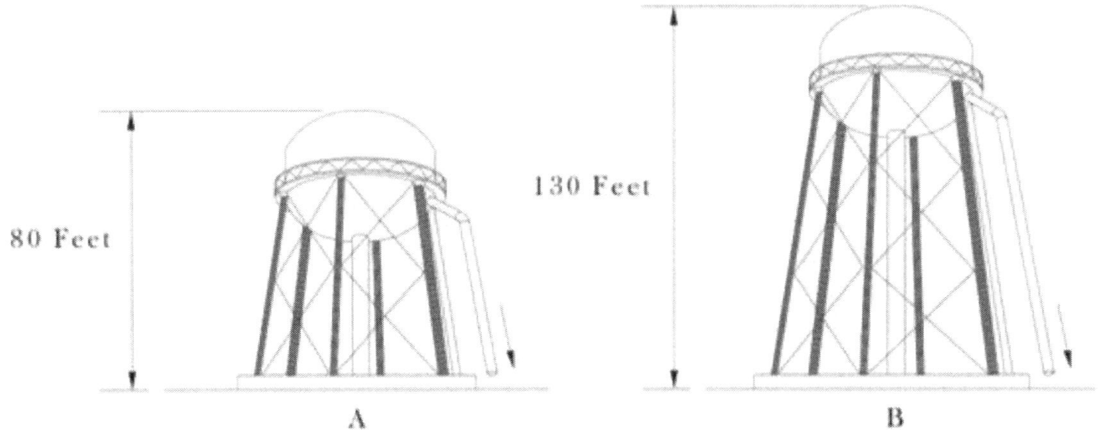

36. The weight of the boxes is resting on a platform suspended in the air by two ropes. Which of the two ropes (A or B) is supporting more of the weight? (If equal, mark C)

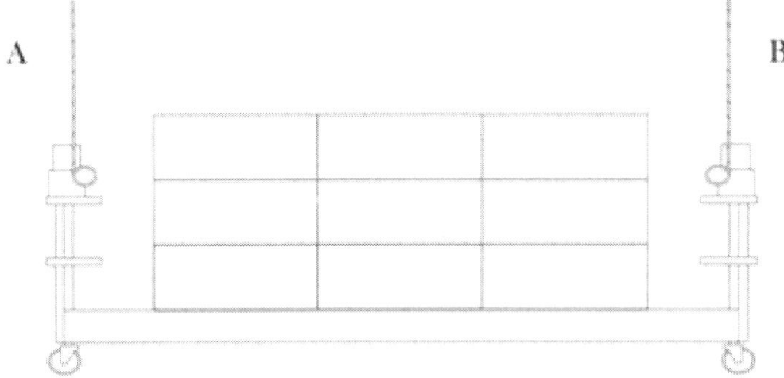

37. Container A contains 100 ml pure water and container B contains 100 ml vinegar. Assume an object is thrown into either container; in which of these two containers is the object more likely to float? (If equal, mark C)

38. Which of the two scenarios (A or B) requires less effort to pull the weight up off the ground? (If equal, mark C)

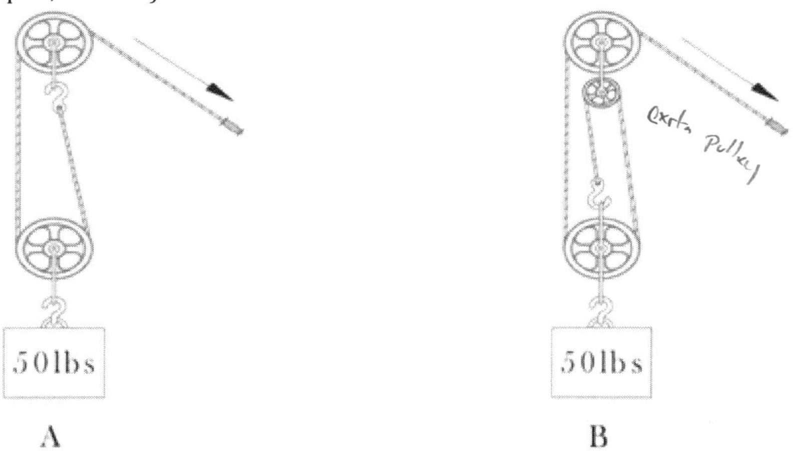

39. In which situation (A or B) will the ball reach the bottom of the ramp quicker? (If equal, mark C)

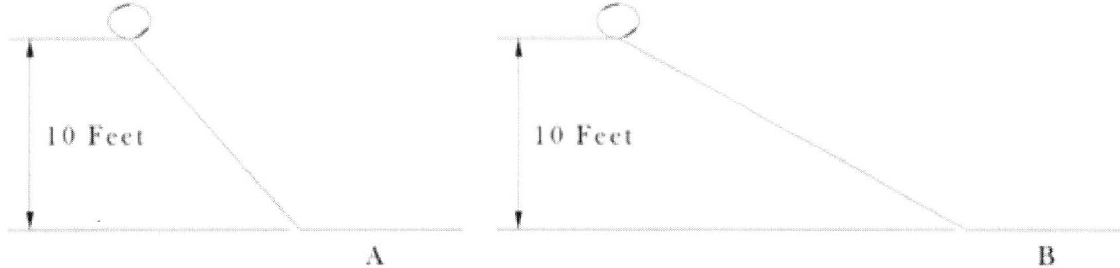

40. Container A holds 1 qt of water and container B holds 1 qt of motor oil. Assume each container is poured down a funnel at the same time. Which of the two contents will reach the bottom of the funnel more quickly? (If equal, mark C)

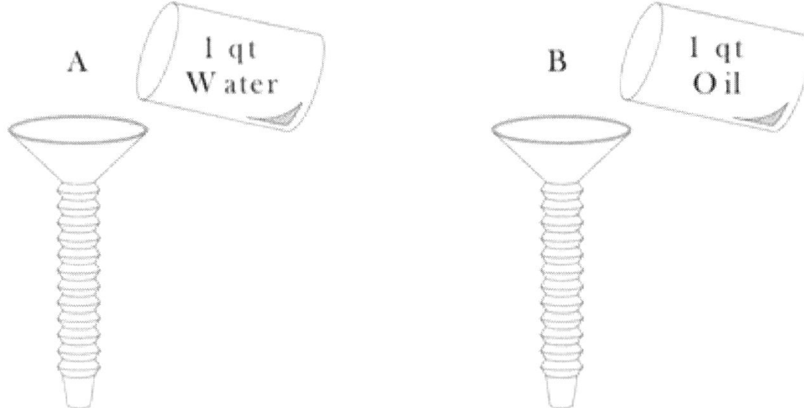

41. A full goblet is attached to the inside of a wheel rotating at a rate of 30 revolutions per second. In which direction (A or B) will the contents of the glass tend to go as the wheel rotates? (If none, mark C)

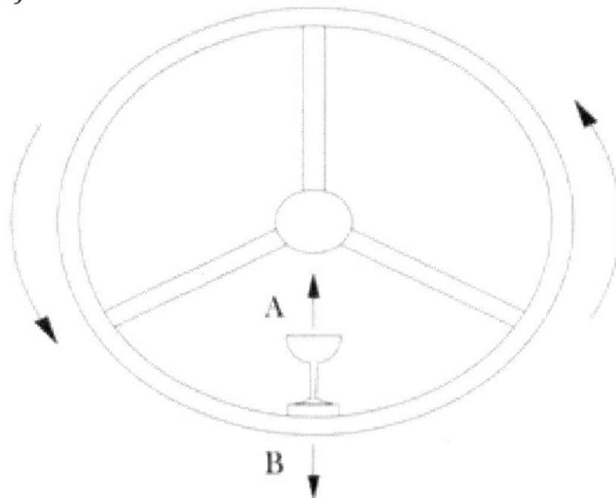

42. Which car (A or B) will travel a greater distance on the given track? (If equal, mark C)

43. In which direction (A or B) will the ball move once the sticks of dynamite explode? (If neither, mark C)

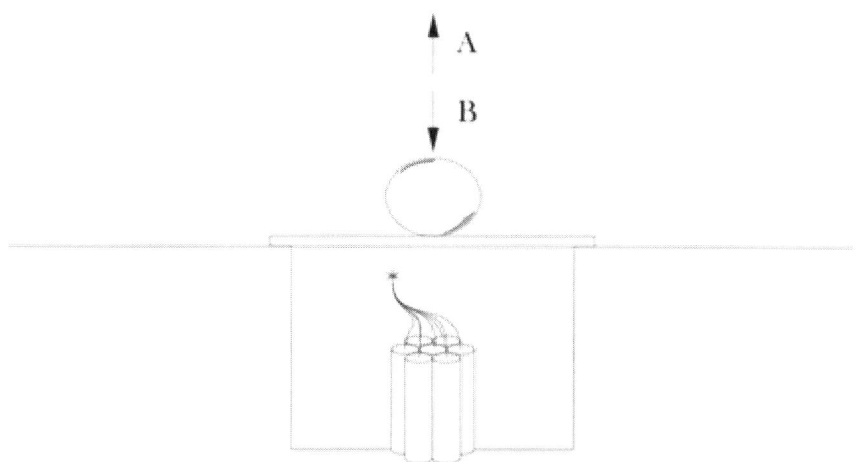

44. In which direction (A or B) will pulley 4 spin if pulley 1 is spinning counter-clockwise? (If none, mark C)

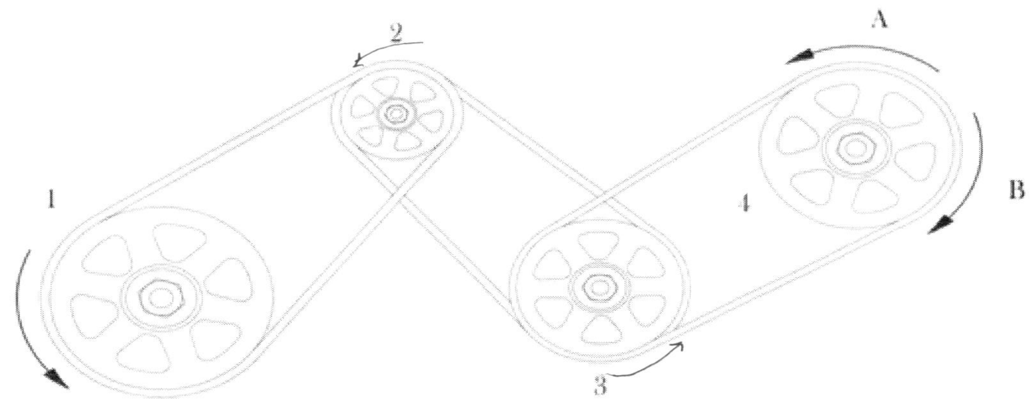

Answers and Explanations

Mathematical Usage

1. D: 13.23 pounds

$$6\ kilograms\ \times \frac{2.205\ pounds}{1\ kilogram} = 13.23\ pounds$$

2. A: 160 rods

$$4\ furlongs \times \frac{40\ rods}{1\ furlong} = 160\ rods$$

3. A: 5 pounds

$$80\ ounces \times \frac{1\ pound}{16\ ounces} = 5\ pounds$$

4. C: 130,680 square feet

$$3\ acres \times \frac{43{,}560\ sq\ ft}{1\ acre} = 130{,}680\ sq\ ft$$

5. B: 3.218 kilometers

$$2\ miles \times \frac{1.609\ kilometers}{1\ mile} = 3.218\ kilometers$$

6. D: 0.75 gallons

$$3\ quarts\ \times \frac{1\ gallon}{4\ quarts} = 0.75\ gallons$$

7. C: 72 feet

$$12\ fathoms \times \frac{6\ feet}{1\ fathom} = 72\ feet$$

8. A: 3 barrels

$$126\ gallons \times \frac{1\ barrel}{42\ gallons} = 3\ barrels$$

9. D: 88 feet/sec

$$60\frac{miles}{hr} \times \frac{4.4\frac{feet}{sec}}{3\frac{mile}{hr}} = 88\frac{feet}{sec}$$

10. B: 0.5 kilograms

$$500\ grams \times \frac{1\ kilogram}{1000\ grams} = 0.5\ kilograms$$

11. D: 150 centimeters

$$15\ hands \times \frac{10\ centimeters}{1\ hand} = 150\ centimeters$$

12. C: 4 gallons

$$15.14\ liters \times \frac{1\ gallon}{3.785\ liters} = 4\ gallons$$

13. A: 336 quarts

$$2\ barrels \times \frac{42\ gallons}{1\ barrel} \times \frac{4\ quarts}{1\ gallon} = 336\ quarts$$

14. B: 160,934 centimeters

$$1\ mile \times \frac{5280\ feet}{1\ mile} \times \frac{12\ inches}{1\ foot} \times \frac{2.54\ centimeters}{1\ inch} = 160{,}934\ centimeters$$

Or, approximately:

$$1\ mile \times \frac{1.609\ kilometers}{1\ mile} \times \frac{100{,}000\ centimeters}{1\ kilometer} = 160{,}900\ centimeters$$

15. D: 6000 grams

$$13.2\ pounds \times \frac{1\ kilogram}{2.2\ pounds} \times \frac{1000\ grams}{1\ kilogram} = 6000\ grams$$

16. C: 576 inches

$$8\ fathoms \times \frac{6\ feet}{1\ fathom} \times \frac{12\ inches}{1\ foot} = 576\ inches$$

17. A: 7.57 liters

$$8\ quarts \times \frac{1\ gallon}{4\ quarts} \times \frac{3.785\ quarts}{1\ gallon} = 7.57\ liters$$

18. C: 152.4 centimeters

$$5\ \text{feet} \times \frac{12\ \text{inches}}{1\ \text{foot}} \times \frac{2.54\ \text{centimeters}}{1\ \text{inch}} = 152.4\ \text{centimeters}$$

Reading for Comprehension

1. A: Solar radiation is not listed as a component of comet nuclei.

2. D: The passage's 5th paragraph notes that some scientists believe that comet collisions with Earth brought a large proportion of Earth's water.

3. B: The second sentence in the passage notes that comets are distinguishable from asteroids by the presence of comas or tails.

4. B: A comet with an orbit of longer than 200 years is a long period comet.

5. C: The third paragraph notes that there are over 3,500 known comets. It also notes that this represents only a small portion of those in existence.

6. A: The first paragraph explains that a coma is made up of released dust and gas.

7. C: The second paragraph notes that because they have low mass, they don't become spherical and have irregular shapes.

8. A: The second paragraph notes that some comets may be tens of kilometers across. It also notes that comas may be larger than the sun.

9. D: The sixth paragraph notes that most comets have oval shaped orbits.

10. D: The first paragraph notes that comets in the outer solar system are difficult to see because they are small.

11. B: Cilia and flagella are both organelles, which are defined in the first paragraph as sub-cellular structures that perform a particular function.

12. A: The second paragraph describes the function of cilia as providing fluid flow across the gills or the epithelia lining the digestive tract. The stomach is part of the digestive tract.

13. C: The third paragraph of the text describes 9 peripheral pairs of polymers, and 2 central ones, or 20 in all.

14. B: Tubulin and dynein are both defined as proteins in the text. Flagellin is a protein, but it is not mentioned in the text. Sonneborn is not a protein; he was a scientist.

15. B: The mechanism is described in detail in the fourth paragraph. Dynein causes the outer polymer pairs to slide past each other, not to bend. The inner polymers do not have dynein associated with them, so they are not involved in the bending. And the passage cites no evidence to suggest that the organelles contract.

16. C: Although the polymers in this passage are made of protein subunits, the definition is more general. The third paragraph tells us that in this case the subunits are tubulin proteins.

17. D: This is mentioned in the first paragraph.

18. C: The first paragraph states that the main purpose of DST it to make better use of daylight.

19. A: Energy conservation is discussed as a possible benefit of DST, not a negative effect of it.

20. D: The first paragraph states that DST involves setting clocks forward one hour in the spring and one hour backward in the fall.

21. B: The last sentence in paragraph four notes that agricultural and evening entertainment interests have historically been opposed to DST.

22. D: The passage gives examples of both good and bad effects extra daylight can have on health.

23. D: The sixth paragraph notes that DST is observed in only some regions of Brazil.

24. C: The last paragraph of the passage notes that DST can lead to peculiar situations, and relays an anecdote about the effect of DST on the birth order of twins.

25. B: In the second paragraph, the author asserts that Benjamin Franklin suggested DST as a way to save candles.

26. C: The second paragraph of the passage notes that "up to one-third of people with peanut allergies have severe reactions." Since one-third is approximately 33%, (C) is the correct choice.

27. D: The second paragraph of the passage notes that in 2008, Duke experts stated that they expect to offer treatment in five years. Five years from 2008 is 2013.

28. B: The last sentence in paragraph five lists the cuisines in which one should watch for peanuts. Italian is not listed.

29. A: The second sentence of the first paragraph states that peanut allergy is the most common cause of food-related death.

30. C: The passage implies that it is not always easy to know which foods have traces of peanuts in them and that it's important to make sure you know what you're eating. This is hard or impossible if you share someone else's food.

31. D: Paragraph two gives examples of symptoms of peanut allergies and, more specifically, examples of symptoms of anaphylaxis. A running or stuffy nose is given as a symptom of the former, but not of the latter.

32. B: The fourth paragraph indicates that a child's odds of developing a peanut allergy are almost 50% when one of the two parents also has a peanut allergy.

Answer Key

Assembly and Mechanical Concepts

Assembly		Mechanical	
Question	Answer	Question	Answer
1.	2	1.	B
2.	3	2.	A
3.	5	3.	A
4.	4	4.	B
5.	3	5.	B
6.	4	6.	C
7.	1	7.	B
8.	2	8.	C
9.	5	9.	A
10.	2	10.	B
11.	4	11.	A
12.	1	12.	B
13.	2	13.	A
14.	5	14.	A
15.	2	15.	B
16.	3	16.	B
17.	5	17.	A
18.	4	18.	A
19.	1	19.	B
20.	2	20.	C
		21.	A
		22.	C
		23.	A
		24.	B
		25.	B
		26.	A
		27.	A
		28.	C
		29.	C
		30.	C
		31.	C
		32.	B
		33.	A
		34.	B
		35.	B
		36.	C
		37.	C
		38.	B
		39.	A

		40.	A
		41.	C
		42.	C
		43.	A
		44.	A

Secret Key #1 - Time is Your Greatest Enemy

Pace Yourself

Wear a watch. At the beginning of the test, check the time (or start a chronometer on your watch to count the minutes), and check the time after every few questions to make sure you are "on schedule."

If you are forced to speed up, do it efficiently. Usually one or more answer choices can be eliminated without too much difficulty. Above all, don't panic. Don't speed up and just begin guessing at random choices. By pacing yourself, and continually monitoring your progress against your watch, you will always know exactly how far ahead or behind you are with your available time. If you find that you are one minute behind on the test, don't skip one question without spending any time on it, just to catch back up. Take 15 fewer seconds on the next four questions, and after four questions you'll have caught back up. Once you catch back up, you can continue working each problem at your normal pace.

Furthermore, don't dwell on the problems that you were rushed on. If a problem was taking up too much time and you made a hurried guess, it must be difficult. The difficult questions are the ones you are most likely to miss anyway, so it isn't a big loss. It is better to end with more time than you need than to run out of time.

Lastly, sometimes it is beneficial to slow down if you are constantly getting ahead of time. You are always more likely to catch a careless mistake by working more slowly than quickly, and among very high-scoring test takers (those who are likely to have lots of time left over), careless errors affect the score more than mastery of material.

Secret Key #2 - Practice Smarter, Not Harder

Many test takers delay the test preparation process because they dread the awful amounts of practice time they think necessary to succeed on the test. We have refined an effective method that will take you only a fraction of the time.

There are a number of "obstacles" in your way to succeed. Among these are answering questions, finishing in time, and mastering test-taking strategies. All must be executed on the day of the test at peak performance, or your score will suffer. The test is a mental marathon that has a large impact on your future.

Just like a marathon runner, it is important to work your way up to the full challenge. So first you just worry about questions, and then time, and finally strategy:

Success Strategy

1. Find a good source for practice tests.
2. If you are willing to make a larger time investment, consider using more than one study guide- often the different approaches of multiple authors will help you "get" difficult concepts.
3. Take a practice test with no time constraints, with all study helps "open book." Take your time with questions and focus on applying strategies.
4. Take a practice test with time

constraints, with all guides "open book."
5. Take a final practice test with no open material and time limits

If you have time to take more practice tests, just repeat step 5. By gradually exposing yourself to the full rigors of the test environment, you will condition your mind to the stress of test day and maximize your success.

Secret Key #3 - **Prepare, Don't** Procrastinate

Let me state an obvious fact: if you take the test three times, you will get three different scores. This is due to the way you feel on test day, the level of preparedness you have, and, despite the test writers' claims to the contrary, some tests WILL be easier for you than others.

Since your future depends so much on your score, you should maximize your chances of success. In order to maximize the likelihood of success, you've got to prepare in advance. This means taking practice tests and spending time learning the information and test taking strategies you will need to succeed.

Never take the test as a "practice" test, expecting that you can just take it again if you need to. Feel free to take sample tests on your own, but when you go to take the official test, be prepared, be focused, and do your best the first time!

Secret Key #4 - Test Yourself

Everyone knows that time is money. There is no need to spend too much of your time or too little of your time preparing for the test. You should only spend as much of your precious time preparing as is necessary for you to get the score you need.

Once you have taken a practice test under real conditions of time constraints, then you will know if you are ready for the test or not.
If you have scored extremely high the first time that you take the practice test, then there is not much point in spending countless hours studying. You are already there.

Benchmark your abilities by retaking practice tests and seeing how much you have improved. Once you score high enough to guarantee success, then you are ready.

If you have scored well below where you need, then knuckle down and begin studying in earnest. Check your improvement regularly through the use of practice tests under real conditions. Above all, don't worry, panic, or give up. The key is perseverance!

Then, when you go to take the test, remain confident and remember how well you did on the practice tests. If you can score high enough on a practice test, then you can do the same on the real thing.

General Strategies

The most important thing you can do is to ignore your fears and jump into the test immediately- do not be overwhelmed by any strange-sounding terms. You have to jump into the test like jumping into a pool- all at once is the easiest way.

Make Predictions

As you read and understand the question, try to guess what the answer will be. Remember that several of the answer choices are wrong, and once you begin reading them, your mind will immediately become cluttered with answer choices designed to throw you off. Your mind is typically the most focused immediately after you have read the question and digested its contents. If you can, try to predict what the correct answer will be. You may be surprised at what you can predict.

Quickly scan the choices and see if your prediction is in the listed answer choices. If it is, then you can be quite confident that you have the right answer. It still won't hurt to check the other answer choices, but most of the time, you've got it!

Answer the Question

It may seem obvious to only pick answer choices that answer the question, but the test writers can create some excellent answer choices that are wrong. Don't pick an answer just because it sounds right, or you believe it to be true. It MUST answer the question. Once you've made your selection, always go back and check it against the question and make sure that you didn't misread the question, and the answer choice does answer the question posed.

Benchmark

After you read the first answer choice, decide if you think it sounds correct or not. If it doesn't, move on to the next answer choice. If it does, mentally mark that answer choice. This doesn't mean that you've definitely selected it as your answer choice, it just means that it's the best you've seen thus far. Go ahead and read the next choice. If the next choice is worse than the one you've already selected, keep going to the next answer choice. If the next choice is better than the choice you've already selected, mentally mark the new answer choice as your best guess.

The first answer choice that you select becomes your standard. Every other answer choice must be benchmarked against that standard. That choice is correct until proven otherwise by another answer choice beating it out. Once you've decided that no other answer choice seems as good, do one final check to ensure that your answer choice answers the question posed.

Valid Information

Don't discount any of the information provided in the question. Every piece of information may be necessary to determine the correct answer. None of the information in the question is there to throw you off (while the answer choices will certainly have information to throw you off). If two seemingly unrelated topics are discussed, don't ignore either. You can be confident there is a relationship, or it wouldn't be included in the question, and you are probably going to have to determine what is that relationship to find the answer.

Avoid "Fact Traps"

Don't get distracted by a choice that is factually true. Your search is for the answer that answers the question. Stay focused and don't fall for an answer that is true but incorrect. Always go back to the question and make sure you're choosing an answer that actually answers the question and is not just a true statement. An answer can be factually correct, but it MUST answer the question asked. Additionally, two answers can both be seemingly correct, so be sure to read all of the answer choices, and make sure that you get the one that BEST answers the question.

Milk the Question

Some of the questions may throw you completely off. They might deal with a subject you have not been exposed to, or one that you haven't reviewed in years. While your lack of knowledge about the subject will be a hindrance, the question itself can give you many clues that will help you find the correct answer. Read the question carefully and look for clues. Watch particularly for adjectives and nouns describing difficult terms or words that you don't recognize. Regardless of if you completely understand a word or not, replacing it with a synonym either provided or one you more familiar with may help you to understand what the questions are asking. Rather than wracking your mind about specific detailed information concerning a difficult term or word, try to use mental substitutes that are easier to understand.

The Trap of Familiarity

Don't just choose a word because you recognize it. On difficult questions, you may not recognize a number of words in the answer choices. The test writers don't put "make-believe" words on the test; so don't think that just because you only recognize all the words in one answer choice means that answer choice must be correct. If you only recognize words in one answer choice, then focus on that one. Is it correct? Try your best to determine if it is correct. If it is, that is great, but if it doesn't, eliminate it. Each word and answer choice you eliminate increases your chances of getting the question correct, even if you then have to guess among the unfamiliar choices.

Eliminate Answers

Eliminate choices as soon as you realize they are wrong. But be careful! Make sure you consider all of the possible answer choices. Just because one appears right, doesn't mean that the next one won't be even better! The test writers will usually put more than one good answer choice for every question, so read all of them. Don't worry if you are stuck between two that seem right. By getting down to just two remaining possible choices, your odds are now 50/50. Rather than wasting too much time, play the odds. You are guessing, but guessing wisely, because you've been able to knock out some of the answer choices that you know are wrong. If you are eliminating choices and realize that the last answer choice you are left with is also obviously wrong, don't panic. Start over and consider each choice again. There may easily be something that you missed the first time and will realize on the second pass.

Tough Questions

If you are stumped on a problem or it appears too hard or too difficult, don't waste time. Move on! Remember though, if you can quickly check for obviously incorrect answer choices, your chances of guessing correctly are greatly improved. Before you completely give up, at least try to knock out a couple of possible answers. Eliminate what you can and then guess at the remaining answer choices before moving on.

Brainstorm

If you get stuck on a difficult question, spend a few seconds quickly brainstorming. Run through the complete list of possible answer choices. Look at each choice and ask yourself, "Could this answer the question satisfactorily?" Go through each answer choice and consider it independently of the other. By systematically going through all possibilities, you may find something that you would otherwise overlook.

Remember that when you get stuck, it's important to try to keep moving.

Read Carefully

Understand the problem. Read the question and answer choices carefully. Don't miss the question because you misread the terms. You have plenty of time to read each question thoroughly and make sure you understand what is being asked. Yet a happy medium must be attained, so don't waste too much time. You must read carefully, but efficiently.

Face Value

When in doubt, use common sense. Always accept the situation in the problem at face value. Don't read too much into it. These problems will not require you to make huge leaps of logic. The test writers aren't trying to throw you off with a cheap trick. If you have to go beyond creativity and make a leap of logic in order to have an answer choice answer the question, then you should look at the other answer choices. Don't overcomplicate the problem by creating theoretical relationships or explanations that will warp time or space. These are normal problems rooted in reality. It's just that the applicable relationship or explanation may not be readily apparent and you have to figure things out. Use your common sense to interpret anything that isn't clear.

Prefixes

If you're having trouble with a word in the question or answer choices, try dissecting it. Take advantage of every clue that the word might include. Prefixes and suffixes can be a huge help. Usually they allow you to determine a basic meaning. Pre- means before, post- means after, pro - is positive, de- is negative. From these prefixes and suffixes, you can get an idea of the general meaning of the word and try to put it into context. Beware though of any traps. Just because con is the opposite of pro, doesn't necessarily mean congress is the opposite of progress!

Hedge Phrases

Watch out for critical "hedge" phrases, such as likely, may, can, will often, sometimes, often, almost, mostly, usually, generally, rarely, sometimes. Question writers insert these hedge phrases to cover every possibility. Often an answer choice will be wrong simply because it leaves no room for exception. Avoid answer choices that have definitive words like "exactly," and "always".

Switchback Words

Stay alert for "switchbacks". These are the words and phrases frequently used to alert you to shifts in thought. The most common switchback word is "but". Others include although, however, nevertheless, on the other hand, even though, while, in spite of, despite, regardless of.

New Information

Correct answer choices will rarely have completely new information included. Answer choices typically are straightforward reflections of the material asked about and will directly relate to the question. If a new piece of information is included in an answer choice that doesn't even seem to relate to the topic being asked about, then that answer choice is likely incorrect. All of the information needed to answer the question is usually provided for you, and so you should not have to make guesses that are unsupported or choose answer choices that require unknown information that cannot be reasoned on its own.

Time Management

On technical questions, don't get lost on

the technical terms. Don't spend too much time on any one question. If you don't know what a term means, then since you don't have a dictionary, odds are you aren't going to get much further. You should immediately recognize terms as whether or not you know them. If you don't, work with the other clues that you have, the other answer choices and terms provided, but don't waste too much time trying to figure out a difficult term.

Contextual Clues

Look for contextual clues. An answer can be right but not correct. The contextual clues will help you find the answer that is most right and is correct. Understand the context in which a phrase or statement is made. This will help you make important distinctions.

Don't Panic

Panicking will not answer any questions for you. Therefore, it isn't helpful. When you first see the question, if your mind goes blank, take a deep breath. Force yourself to mechanically go through the steps of solving the problem and using the strategies you've learned.

Pace Yourself

Don't get clock fever. It's easy to be overwhelmed when you're looking at a page full of questions, your mind is full of random thoughts and feeling confused, and the clock is ticking down faster than you would like. Calm down and maintain the pace that you have set for yourself. As long as you are on track by monitoring your pace, you are guaranteed to have enough time for yourself. When you get to the last few minutes of the test, it may seem like you won't have enough time left, but if you only have as many questions as you should have left at that point, then you're right on track!

Answer Selection

The best way to pick an answer choice is to eliminate all of those that are wrong, until only one is left and confirm that is the correct answer. Sometimes though, an answer choice may immediately look right. Be careful! Take a second to make sure that the other choices are not equally obvious. Don't make a hasty mistake. There are only two times that you should stop before checking other answers. First is when you are positive that the answer choice you have selected is correct. Second is when time is almost out and you have to make a quick guess!

Check Your Work

Since you will probably not know every term listed and the answer to every question, it is important that you get credit for the ones that you do know. Don't miss any questions through careless mistakes. If at all possible, try to take a second to look back over your answer selection and make sure you've selected the correct answer choice and haven't made a costly careless mistake (such as marking an answer choice that you didn't mean to mark). This quick double check should more than pay for itself in caught mistakes for the time it costs.

Beware of Directly Quoted Answers

Sometimes an answer choice will repeat word for word a portion of the question or reference section. However, beware of such exact duplication – it may be a trap! More than likely, the correct choice will paraphrase or summarize a point, rather than being exactly the same wording.

Slang

Scientific sounding answers are better than slang ones. An answer choice that begins "To compare the outcomes…" is much more likely to be correct than one that begins "Because some people insisted…"

Extreme Statements

Avoid wild answers that throw out highly controversial ideas that are proclaimed as established fact. An answer choice that states the "process should be used in certain situations, if…" is much more likely to be correct than one that states the "process should be discontinued completely." The first is a calm rational statement and doesn't even make a definitive, uncompromising stance, using a hedge word "if" to provide wiggle room, whereas the second choice is a radical idea and far more extreme.

Answer Choice Families

When you have two or more answer choices that are direct opposites or parallels, one of them is usually the correct answer. For instance, if one answer choice states "x increases" and another answer choice states "x decreases" or "y increases," then those two or three answer choices are very similar in construction and fall into the same family of answer choices. A family of answer choices is when two or three answer choices are very similar in construction, and yet often have a directly opposite meaning. Usually the correct answer choice will be in that family of answer choices. The "odd man out" or answer choice that doesn't seem to fit the parallel construction of the other answer choices is more likely to be incorrect.

Special Report: How to Overcome Test Anxiety

The very nature of tests caters to some level of anxiety, nervousness or tension, just as we feel for any important event that occurs in our lives. A little bit of anxiety or nervousness can be a good thing. It helps us with motivation, and makes achievement just that much sweeter. However, too much anxiety can be a problem; especially if it hinders our ability to function and perform.

"Test anxiety," is the term that refers to the emotional reactions that some test-takers experience when faced with a test or exam. Having a fear of testing and exams is based upon a rational fear, since the test-taker's performance can shape the course of an academic career. Nevertheless, experiencing excessive fear of examinations will only interfere with the test-takers ability to perform, and his/her chances to be successful.

There are a large variety of causes that can contribute to the development and sensation of test anxiety. These include, but are not limited to lack of performance and worrying about issues surrounding the test.

Lack of Preparation

Lack of preparation can be identified by the following behaviors or situations:

Not scheduling enough time to study, and therefore cramming the night before the test or exam
Managing time poorly, to create the sensation that there is not enough time to do everything
Failing to organize the text information in advance, so that the study material consists of the entire text and not simply the pertinent information
Poor overall studying habits

Worrying, on the other hand, can be related to both the test taker, or many other factors around him/her that will be affected by the results of the test. These include worrying about:

Previous performances on similar exams, or exams in general
How friends and other students are achieving
The negative consequences that will result from a poor grade or failure

There are three primary elements to test anxiety. Physical components, which involve the same typical bodily reactions as those to acute anxiety (to be discussed below). Emotional factors have to do with fear or panic. Mental or cognitive issues concerning attention spans and memory abilities.

Physical Signals

There are many different symptoms of test anxiety, and these are not limited to mental and emotional strain. Frequently there are a range of physical signals that will let a test taker know that he/she is suffering from test anxiety. These bodily changes can include the following:

Perspiring
Sweaty palms
Wet, trembling hands
Nausea
Dry mouth
A knot in the stomach
Headache
Faintness
Muscle tension
Aching shoulders, back and neck
Rapid heart beat
Feeling too hot/cold

To recognize the sensation of test anxiety, a test-taker should monitor him/herself for the following sensations:

The physical distress symptoms as listed above
Emotional sensitivity, expressing emotional feelings such as the need to cry or laugh too much, or a sensation of anger or helplessness
A decreased ability to think, causing the test-taker to blank out or have racing thoughts that are hard to organize or control.

Though most students will feel some level of anxiety when faced with a test or exam, the majority can cope with that anxiety and maintain it at a manageable level. However, those who cannot are faced with a very real and very serious condition, which can and should be controlled for the immeasurable benefit of this sufferer.

Naturally, these sensations lead to negative results for the testing experience. The most common effects of test anxiety have to do with nervousness and mental blocking.

Nervousness

Nervousness can appear in several different levels:

The test-taker's difficulty, or even inability to read and understand the questions on the test
The difficulty or inability to organize thoughts to a coherent form
The difficulty or inability to recall key words and concepts relating to the testing questions (especially essays)
The receipt of poor grades on a test, though the test material was well known by the test taker

Conversely, a person may also experience mental blocking, which involves:

Blanking out on test questions
Only remembering the correct answers to the questions when the test has already finished.

Fortunately for test anxiety sufferers, beating these feelings, to a large degree, has to do with proper preparation. When a test taker has a feeling of preparedness, then anxiety will be dramatically lessened.

The first step to resolving anxiety issues is to distinguish which of the two types of anxiety are being suffered. If the anxiety is a direct result of a lack of preparation, this should be considered a normal reaction, and the anxiety level (as opposed to the test results) shouldn't be anything to worry about. However, if, when adequately prepared, the test-taker still panics, blanks out, or seems to overreact, this is not a fully rational reaction. While this can be considered normal too, there are many ways to combat and overcome these effects.

Remember that anxiety cannot be entirely eliminated, however, there are ways to minimize it, to make the anxiety easier to manage. Preparation is one of the best ways to minimize test anxiety. Therefore the following techniques are wise in order to best fight off any anxiety that may want to build.

To begin with, try to avoid cramming before a test, whenever it is possible. By trying to memorize an entire term's worth of information in one day, you'll be shocking your system, and not giving yourself a very good chance to absorb the information. This is an easy path to anxiety, so for those who suffer from test anxiety, cramming should not even be considered an option.

Instead of cramming, work throughout the semester to combine all of the material which is presented throughout the semester, and work on it gradually as the course goes by, making sure to master the main concepts first, leaving minor details for a week or so before the test.

To study for the upcoming exam, be sure to pose questions that may be on the examination, to gauge the ability to answer them by integrating the ideas from your texts, notes and lectures, as well as any supplementary readings.

If it is truly impossible to cover all of the information that was covered in that particular term, concentrate on the most important portions, that can be covered very well. Learn these concepts as best as possible, so that when the test comes, a goal can be made to use these concepts as presentations of your knowledge.

In addition to study habits, changes in attitude are critical to beating a struggle with test anxiety. In fact, an improvement of the perspective over the entire test-taking experience can actually help a test taker to enjoy studying and therefore improve the overall experience. Be certain not to overemphasize the significance of the grade - know that the result of the test is neither a reflection of self worth, nor is it a measure of intelligence; one grade will not predict a person's future success.

To improve an overall testing outlook, the following steps should be tried:

Keeping in mind that the most reasonable expectation for taking a test is to expect to try to demonstrate as much of what you know as you possibly can.
Reminding ourselves that a test is only one test; this is not the only one, and there will be others.
The thought of thinking of oneself in an irrational, all-or-nothing term should be avoided at all costs.
A reward should be designated for after the test, so there's something to look forward to. Whether it be going to a movie, going out to eat, or simply visiting friends, schedule it in advance, and do it no matter what result is expected on the exam.

Test-takers should also keep in mind that the basics are some of the most important things, even beyond anti-anxiety techniques and studying. Never neglect the basic social, emotional and biological needs, in order to try to absorb information. In order to best achieve, these three factors must be held as just as important as the studying itself.

Study Steps

Remember the following important steps for studying:

Maintain healthy nutrition and exercise habits. Continue both your recreational activities and social pass times. These both contribute to your physical and emotional well being.
Be certain to get a good amount of sleep, especially the night before the test, because when you're overtired you are not able to perform to the best of your best ability.
Keep the studying pace to a moderate level by taking breaks when they are needed, and varying the work whenever possible, to keep the mind fresh instead of getting bored.
When enough studying has been done that all the material that can be learned has been learned, and the test taker is prepared for the test, stop studying and do something relaxing such as listening to music, watching a movie, or taking a warm bubble bath.

There are also many other techniques to minimize the uneasiness or apprehension that is experienced along with test anxiety before, during, or even after the examination. In fact, there are a great deal of things that can be done to stop anxiety from interfering with lifestyle and performance. Again, remember that anxiety will not be eliminated entirely, and it shouldn't be. Otherwise that "up" feeling for exams would not exist, and most of us depend on that sensation to perform better than usual. However, this anxiety has to be at a level that is manageable.

Of course, as we have just discussed, being prepared for the exam is half the battle right away. Attending all classes, finding out what knowledge will be expected on the exam, and knowing the exam schedules are easy steps to lowering anxiety. Keeping up with work will remove the need to cram, and efficient study habits will eliminate wasted time. Studying should be done in an ideal location for concentration, so that it is simple to become interested in the material and give it complete attention. A method such as SQ3R (Survey, Question, Read, Recite, Review) is a wonderful key to follow to make sure that the study habits are as effective as possible, especially in the case of learning from a textbook. Flashcards are great techniques for memorization. Learning to take good notes will mean that notes will be full of useful information, so that less sifting will need to be done to seek out what is pertinent for studying. Reviewing notes after class and then again on occasion will keep the information fresh in the mind. From notes that have been taken summary sheets and outlines can be made for simpler reviewing.

A study group can also be a very motivational and helpful place to study, as there will be a sharing of ideas, all of the minds can work together, to make sure that everyone understands, and the studying will be made more interesting because it will be a social occasion.

Basically, though, as long as the test-taker remains organized and self confident, with efficient study habits, less time will need to be spent studying, and higher grades will be achieved.

To become self confident, there are many useful steps. The first of these is "self talk." It has been shown through extensive research, that self-talk for students who suffer from test anxiety, should be well monitored, in order to make sure that it contributes to self confidence as opposed to sinking the student. Frequently the self talk of test-anxious students is negative or self-defeating, thinking that everyone else is smarter and faster, that they always mess up, and that if they don't do well, they'll fail the entire course. It is important to decreasing anxiety that awareness is made of self talk. Try writing any negative self thoughts and then disputing them with a positive statement instead. Begin self-encouragement as though it was a friend speaking. Repeat positive statements to help reprogram the mind to believing in successes instead of failures.

Helpful Techniques

Other extremely helpful techniques include:

Self-visualization of doing well and reaching goals
While aiming for an "A" level of understanding, don't try to "overprotect" by setting your expectations lower. This will only convince the mind to stop studying in order to meet the lower expectations.
Don't make comparisons with the results or habits of other students. These are individual factors, and different things work for different people, causing different results.
Strive to become an expert in learning what works well, and what can be done in order to improve. Consider collecting this data in a journal.
Create rewards for after studying instead of doing things before studying that will only turn into avoidance behaviors.
Make a practice of relaxing - by using methods such as progressive relaxation, self-hypnosis, guided imagery, etc - in order to make relaxation an automatic sensation.
Work on creating a state of relaxed concentration so that concentrating will take on the focus of the mind, so that none will be wasted on worrying.
Take good care of the physical self by eating well and getting enough sleep.
Plan in time for exercise and stick to this plan.

Beyond these techniques, there are other methods to be used before, during and after the test that will help the test-taker perform well in addition to overcoming anxiety.

Before the exam comes the academic preparation. This involves establishing a study schedule and beginning at least one week before the actual date of the test. By doing this, the anxiety of not having enough time to study for the test will be automatically eliminated. Moreover, this will make the studying a much more effective experience, ensuring that the learning will be an easier process. This relieves much undue pressure on the test-taker.

Summary sheets, note cards, and flash cards with the main concepts and examples of these main concepts should be prepared in advance of the actual studying time. A topic should never be eliminated from this process. By omitting a topic because it isn't expected to be on the test is only setting up the test-taker for anxiety should it actually appear on the exam. Utilize the course syllabus for laying out the topics that should be studied. Carefully go over the notes that were made in class, paying special attention to any of the issues that the professor took special care to emphasize while lecturing in class. In the textbooks, use the chapter review, or if possible, the chapter tests, to begin your review.

It may even be possible to ask the instructor what information will be covered on the exam, or what the format of the exam will be (for example, multiple choice, essay, free form, true-false). Additionally, see if it is possible to find out how many questions will be on the test. If a review sheet or sample test has been offered by the professor, make good use of it, above anything else, for the preparation for the test. Another great resource for getting to know the examination is reviewing tests from previous semesters. Use these tests to review, and aim to achieve a 100% score on each of the possible topics. With a few exceptions, the goal that you set for yourself is the highest one that you will reach.

Take all of the questions that were assigned as homework, and rework them to any other possible course material. The more problems reworked, the more skill and confidence will form as a result. When forming the solution to a problem, write out each of the steps. Don't simply do head work. By doing as many steps on paper as possible, much clarification and therefore confidence will be formed. Do this with as many homework problems as possible, before checking the answers. By checking the answer after each problem, a reinforcement will exist, that will not be on the exam. Study situations should be as exam-like as possible, to prime the test-taker's system for the experience. By waiting to check the answers at the end, a psychological advantage will be formed, to decrease the stress factor.

Another fantastic reason for not cramming is the avoidance of confusion in concepts, especially when it comes to mathematics. 8-10 hours of study will become one hundred percent more effective if it is spread out over a week or at least several days, instead of doing it all in one sitting. Recognize that the human brain requires time in order to assimilate new material, so frequent breaks and a span of study time over several days will be much more beneficial.

Additionally, don't study right up until the point of the exam. Studying should stop a minimum of one hour before the exam begins. This allows the brain to rest and put things in their proper order. This will also provide the time to become as relaxed as possible when going into the examination room. The test-taker will also have time to eat well and eat sensibly. Know that the brain needs food as much as the rest of the body. With enough food and enough sleep, as well as a relaxed attitude, the body and the mind are primed for success.

Avoid any anxious classmates who are talking about the exam. These students only spread anxiety, and are not worth sharing the anxious sentimentalities.

Before the test also involves creating a positive attitude, so mental preparation should also be a point of concentration. There are many keys to creating a positive attitude. Should fears become rushing in, make a visualization of taking the exam, doing well, and seeing an A written on the paper. Write out a list of affirmations that will bring a feeling of confidence, such as "I am doing well in my English class," "I studied well and know my material," "I enjoy this class." Even if the affirmations aren't believed at first, it sends a positive message to the subconscious which will result in an alteration of the overall belief system, which is the system that creates reality.

If a sensation of panic begins, work with the fear and imagine the very worst! Work through the entire scenario of not passing the test, failing the entire course, and dropping out of school, followed by not getting a job, and pushing a shopping cart through the dark alley where you'll live. This will place things into perspective! Then, practice deep breathing and create a visualization of the opposite situation - achieving an "A" on the exam, passing the entire course, receiving the degree at a graduation ceremony.

On the day of the test, there are many things to be done to ensure the best results, as well as the most calm outlook. The following stages are suggested in order to maximize test-taking potential:

Begin the examination day with a moderate breakfast, and avoid any coffee or beverages with caffeine if the test taker is prone to jitters. Even people who are used to managing caffeine can feel jittery or light-headed when it is taken on a test day.

Attempt to do something that is relaxing before the examination begins. As last minute cramming clouds the mastering of overall concepts, it is better to use this time to create a calming outlook.

Be certain to arrive at the test location well in advance, in order to provide time to select a location that is away from doors, windows and other distractions, as well as giving enough time to relax before the test begins.

Keep away from anxiety generating classmates who will upset the sensation of stability and relaxation that is being attempted before the exam.

Should the waiting period before the exam begins cause anxiety, create a self-distraction by reading a light magazine or something else that is relaxing and simple.

During the exam itself, read the entire exam from beginning to end, and find out how much time should be allotted to each individual problem. Once writing the exam, should more time be taken for a problem, it should be abandoned, in order to begin another problem. If there is time at the end, the unfinished problem can always be returned to and completed.

Read the instructions very carefully - twice - so that unpleasant surprises won't follow during or after the exam has ended.

When writing the exam, pretend that the situation is actually simply the completion of homework within a library, or at home. This will assist in forming a relaxed atmosphere, and will allow the brain extra focus for the complex thinking function.

Begin the exam with all of the questions with which the most confidence is felt. This will build the confidence level regarding the entire exam and will begin a quality momentum. This will also create encouragement for trying the problems where uncertainty resides.

Going with the "gut instinct" is always the way to go when solving a problem. Second guessing should be avoided at all costs. Have confidence in the ability to do well.

For essay questions, create an outline in advance that will keep the mind organized and make certain that all of the points are remembered. For multiple choice, read every answer, even if the correct one has been spotted - a better one may exist.

Continue at a pace that is reasonable and not rushed, in order to be able to work carefully. Provide enough time to go over the answers at the end, to check for small errors that can be corrected.

Should a feeling of panic begin, breathe deeply, and think of the feeling of the body releasing sand through its pores. Visualize a calm, peaceful place, and include all of the sights, sounds and sensations of this image. Continue the deep breathing, and take a few minutes to continue this with closed eyes. When all is well again, return to the test.

If a "blanking" occurs for a certain question, skip it and move on to the next question. There will be time to return to the other question later. Get everything done that can be done, first, to guarantee all the grades that can be compiled, and to build all of the confidence possible. Then return to the weaker questions to build the marks from there. Remember, one's own reality can be created, so as long as the belief is there, success will follow. And remember: anxiety can happen later, right now, there's an exam to be written!

After the examination is complete, whether there is a feeling for a good grade or a bad grade, don't dwell on the exam, and be certain to follow through on the reward that was promised...and enjoy it! Don't dwell on any mistakes that have been made, as there is nothing that can be done at this point anyway.

Additionally, don't begin to study for the next test right away. Do something relaxing for a while, and let the mind relax and prepare itself to begin absorbing information again.

From the results of the exam - both the grade and the entire experience, be certain to learn from what has gone on. Perfect studying habits and work some more on confidence in order to make the next examination experience even better than the last one.

Learn to avoid places where openings occurred for laziness, procrastination and day dreaming.

Use the time between this exam and the next one to better learn to relax, even learning to relax on cue, so that any anxiety can be controlled during the next exam. Learn how to relax the body. Slouch in your chair if that helps. Tighten and then relax all of the different muscle groups, one group at a time, beginning with the feet and then working all the way up to the neck and face. This will ultimately relax the muscles more than they were to begin with. Learn how to breathe deeply and comfortably, and focus on this breathing going in and out as a relaxing thought. With every exhale, repeat the word "relax."

As common as test anxiety is, it is very possible to overcome it. Make yourself one of the test-takers who overcome this frustrating hindrance.

Special Report: Retaking the Test: What Are Your Chances at Improving Your Score?

After going through the experience of taking a major test, many test takers feel that once is enough. The test usually comes during a period of transition in the test taker's life, and taking the test is only one of a series of important events. With so many distractions and conflicting recommendations, it may be difficult for a test taker to rationally determine whether or not he should retake the test after viewing his scores.

The importance of the test usually only adds to the burden of the retake decision. However, don't be swayed by emotion. There a few simple questions that you can ask yourself to guide you as you try to determine whether a retake would improve your score:

1. What went wrong? Why wasn't your score what you expected?

Can you point to a single factor or problem that you feel caused the low score? Were you sick on test day? Was there an emotional upheaval in your life that caused a distraction? Were you late for the test or not able to use the full time allotment? If you can point to any of these specific, individual problems, then a retake should definitely be considered.

2. Is there enough time to improve?

Many problems that may show up in your score report may take a lot of time for improvement. A deficiency in a particular math skill may require weeks or months of tutoring and studying to improve. If you have enough time to improve an identified weakness, then a retake should definitely be considered.

3. How will additional scores be used? Will a score average, highest score, or most recent score be used?

Different test scores may be handled completely differently. If you've taken the test multiple times, sometimes your highest score is used, sometimes your average score is computed and used, and sometimes your most recent score is used. Make sure you understand what method will be used to evaluate your scores, and use that to help you determine whether a retake should be considered.

4. Are my practice test scores significantly higher than my actual test score?

If you have taken a lot of practice tests and are consistently scoring at a much higher level than your actual test score, then you should consider a retake. However, if you've taken five practice tests and only one of your scores was higher than your actual test score, or if your practice test scores were only slightly higher than your actual test score, then it is unlikely that you will significantly increase your score.

5. Do I need perfect scores or will I be able to live with this score? Will this score still allow me to follow my dreams?

What kind of score is acceptable to you? Is your current score "good enough?" Do you have to have a certain score in order to pursue the future of your dreams? If you won't be happy with your current score, and there's no way that you could live with it, then you should consider a retake. However, don't get your hopes up. If you are looking for significant improvement, that may or may not be possible. But if you won't be happy otherwise, it is at least worth the effort.

Remember that there are other considerations. To achieve your dream, it is likely that your grades may also be taken into account. A great test score is usually not the only thing necessary to succeed. Make sure that you aren't overemphasizing the importance of a high test score.

Furthermore, a retake does not always result in a higher score. Some test takers will score lower on a retake, rather than higher. One study shows that one-fourth of test takers will achieve a significant improvement in test score, while one-sixth of test takers will actually show a decrease. While this shows that most test takers will improve, the majority will only improve their scores a little and a retake may not be worth the test taker's effort.

Finally, if a test is taken only once and is considered in the added context of good grades on the part of a test taker, the person reviewing the grades and scores may be tempted to assume that the test taker just had a bad day while taking the test, and may discount the low test score in favor of the high grades. But if the test is retaken and the scores are approximately the same, then the validity of the low scores are only confirmed. Therefore, a retake could actually hurt a test taker by definitely bracketing a test taker's score ability to a limited range.

Special Report: Additional Bonus Material

Due to our efforts to try to keep this book to a manageable length, we've created a link that will give you access to all of your additional bonus material.

Please visit http://www.mometrix.com/bonus948/mass to access the information.